MOMENTARY ARTIFACTS

PHOTOS BY PETER J. NEBERGALL

AuthorHouse™
1663 Liberty Drive, Suite 200
Bloomington, IN 47403
www.authorhouse.com
Phone: 1-800-839-8640

First published by AuthorHouse 01/10/2008

ISBN: 978-1-4343-5331-3 (sc)

Printed in the United States of America
Bloomington, Indiana

This book is printed on acid-free paper.

This Book is dedicated to the Family: Ginger, Grace, Grainger, Graham, George, and Mr. Sox; to the friends they brought home with them, and to the joy I've always had just watching them be themselves. You're in here, cats!

Peter

Words and Pictures
PO Box 754
Columbia, MO 65205, USA
(573) 864-1563
iusar4s@juno.com

INTRODUCTION

Peter

Peter Nebergall is a traditional photographer. Trained by an associate of Joe Rosenthal, he learned profound regard for the ways and the masters of the 1930s.

Committed to using film (he calls digital photography "Pasteurized processed imitation photography-flavored product"), he prefers his cameras German, and ideally of his own age or older. "The most you can do with newer equipment," he asserts, "is perhaps duplicate what was achieved in 1939 with a Contax, a Rollei, or a Leica. So who really needs the new stuff?"

Bel Canto

Every day, the media bombard us with dark, violent, depressing images of a world seemingly slipping out of our control. Many otherwise fine photographers seem to believe the monotonous repetition of such negativity will spur desired action against that negativity. Are they correct? Or does the steady drumbeat of depression merely jade us, leaving us ever more hardened to the very suffering it depicts?

Hugo Van Lawick wrote that the photographer had a duty to uplift, to inspire, to remind the viewer there still is beauty, still is joy, still is reason for hope.

Peter Nebergall believes this. Taking his cue from the "lyrical documentary" of mentor Walker Evans, he searches for moments of sweetness, of joy, of humor -- and tries to catch them for posterity.

Two Ways

It is accepted that the photographer modifies his environment by his presence. Especially true in the act of portraiture, some lensmen seek to dominate that environment, forcing their subject to react to their presence. Others, taking the opposite tack, work hard to be unobtrusive, trying to limit the change their presence brings.

Peter belongs to the second school. Given a choice, he prefers to keep his own presence minimal. "I don't want you to look at my work and think of *me*," he insists. "I want you to look at the artifact, my picture, and *see the moment I saw*."

Equipment

Although Peter does own some reasonably modern cameras (Leica M2, Nikon F5 and FM2N), he has done some of his best work with old Contax II and III, screw mount Leica, Canon Vt and 7, Rolleicords and Rolleiflexes, Zeiss Super Ikonta, and a profound collection of Exaktas. They all work.

"When Joe Nikons clunks into view," he writes in his *Faces of Punk*, "people's natural reaction is to freeze up, or else to clown, to parody, giving the photographer what they think he wants. My ancient pieces inspire curiosity instead, helping me build a bridge instead of a wall. Portrait photography is a conversation, not an act of theft, and my antiques help further that conversation."

What's his favorite? Hard to say, but he still has (and regularly uses) the Nikkormat EL he bought in 1985, and Leica IIIa he purchased in 1967, and dozens of other ancient machines, spanning formats from 35mm to 4x5.

But it's really about the pictures, now, isn't it?

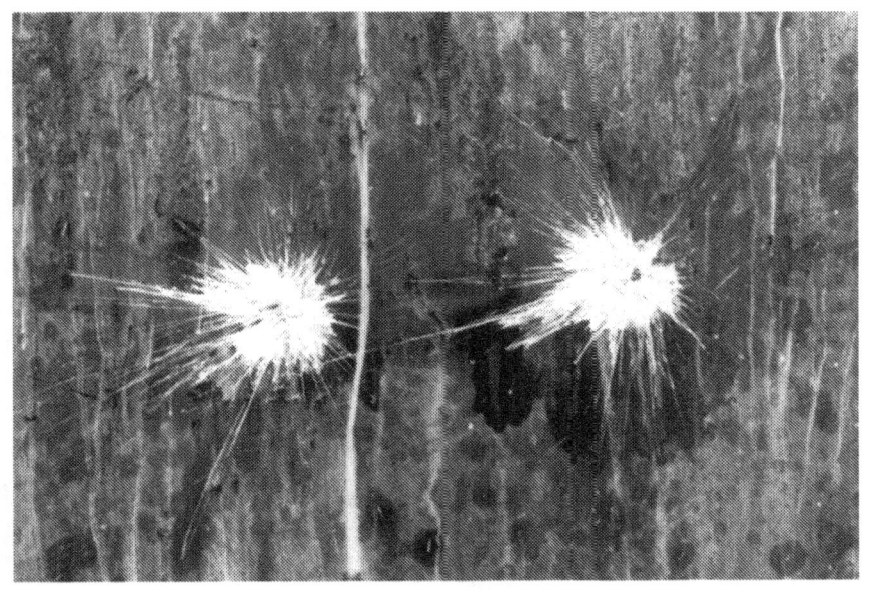

Paintball; Columbia, Missouri, 2004.

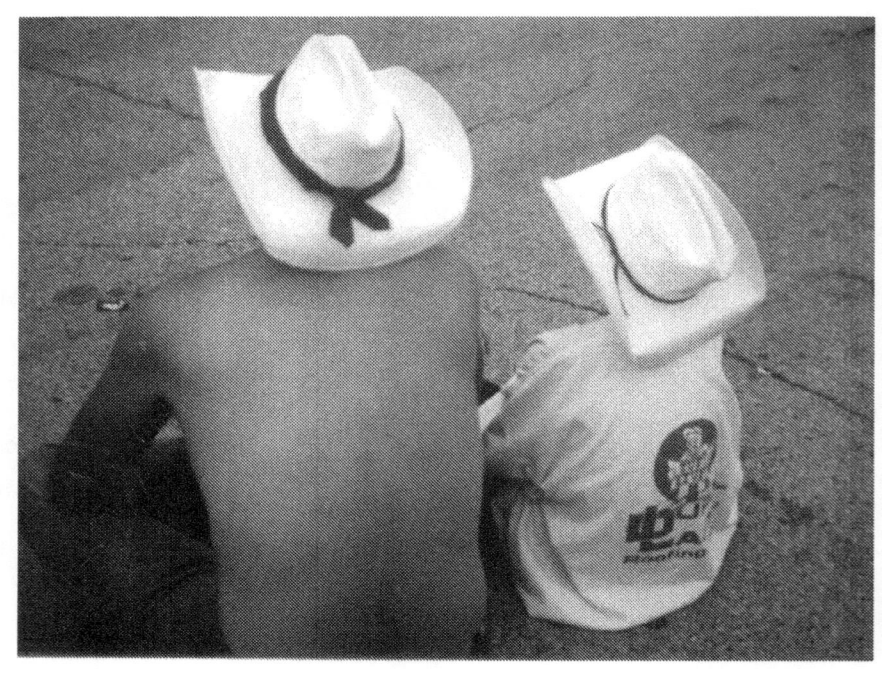

"Like Father, Like Son." Hannibal, Missouri, 2005.

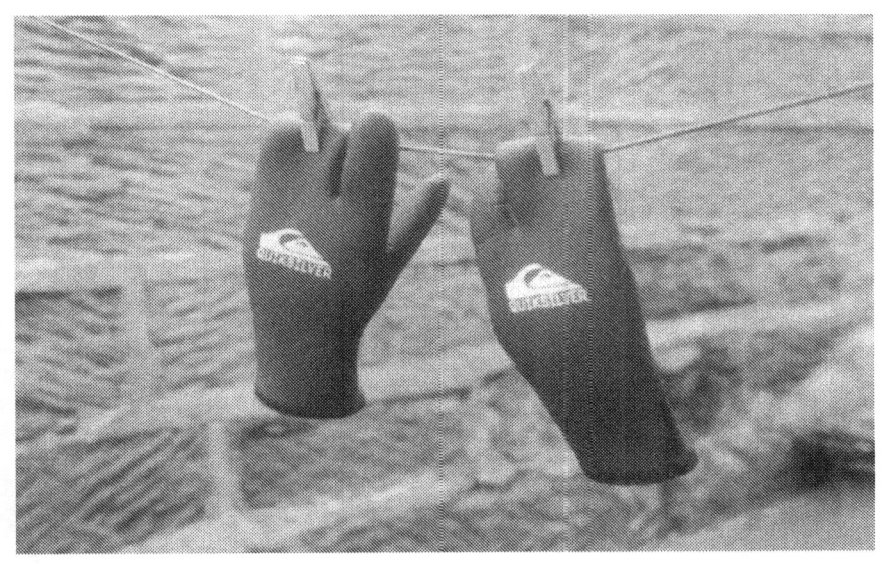

Wet-Suit Mittens, UK, 2002.
No, they're not boxing gloves...

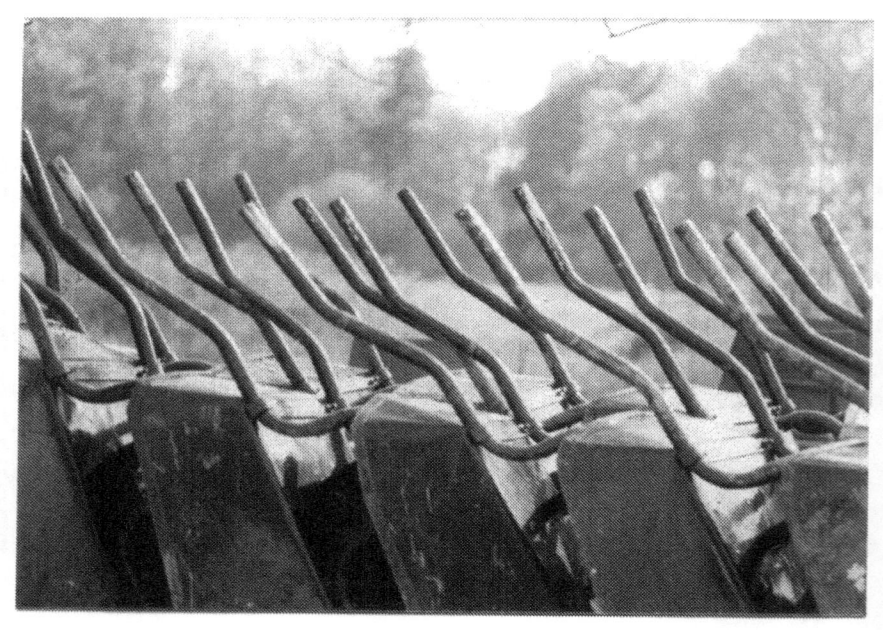

Parked Wheelbarrows, UK, 1984.

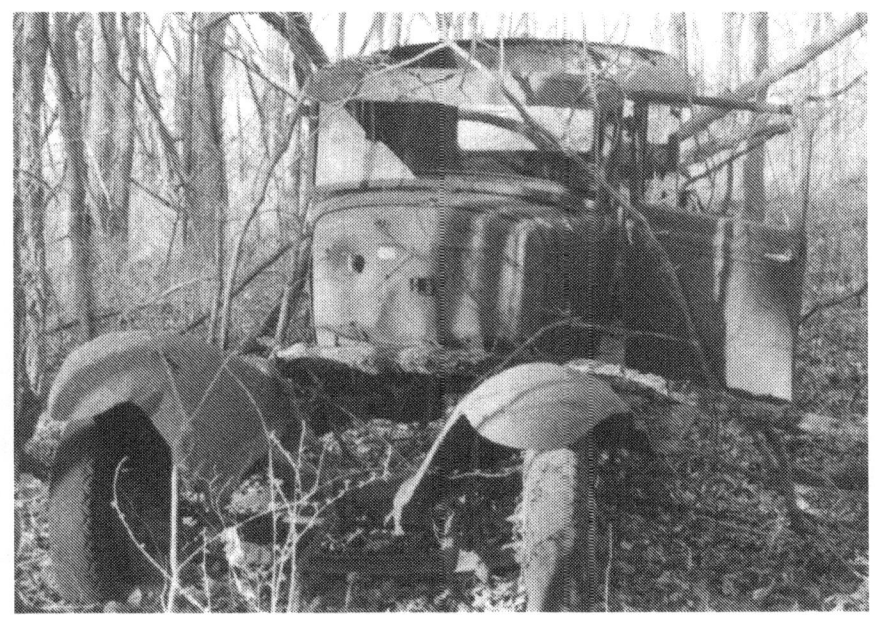

1934 Studebaker Pickup; near my farm in rural Missouri, 2005.

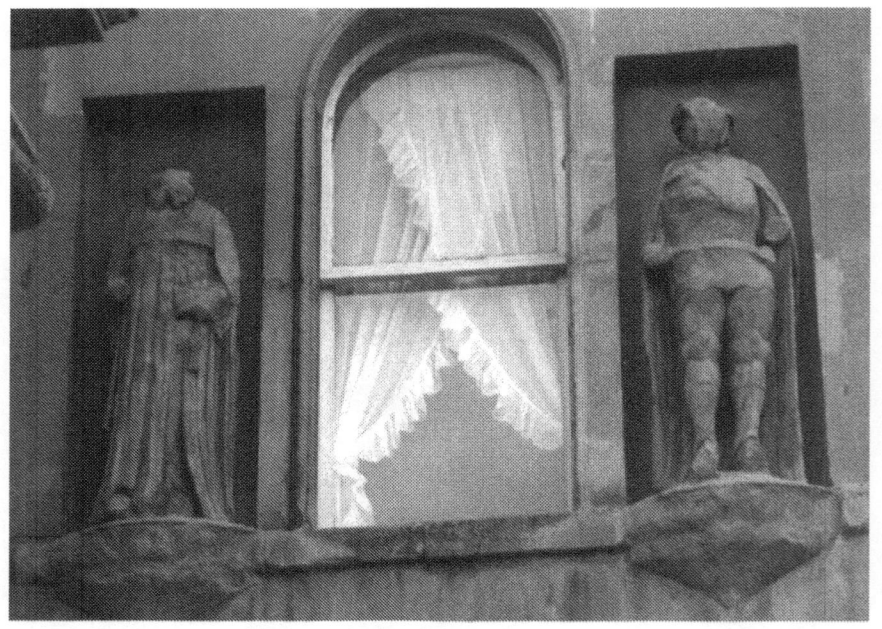

Acid-Rain Damage; Bath, England, 1984. The 500 year old building and its statues are limestone, and in the polluted air, you can almost hear them melting away...

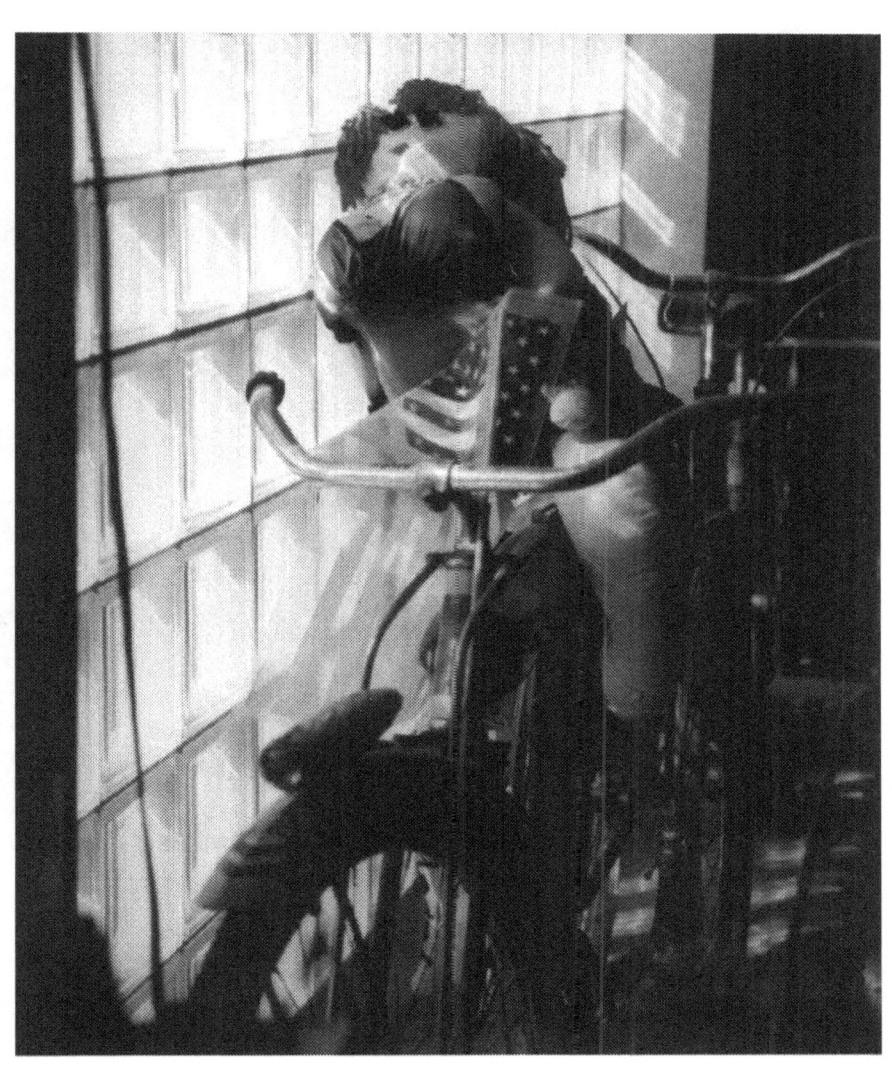

Old Doll, Cincinnati, Ohio, 2007

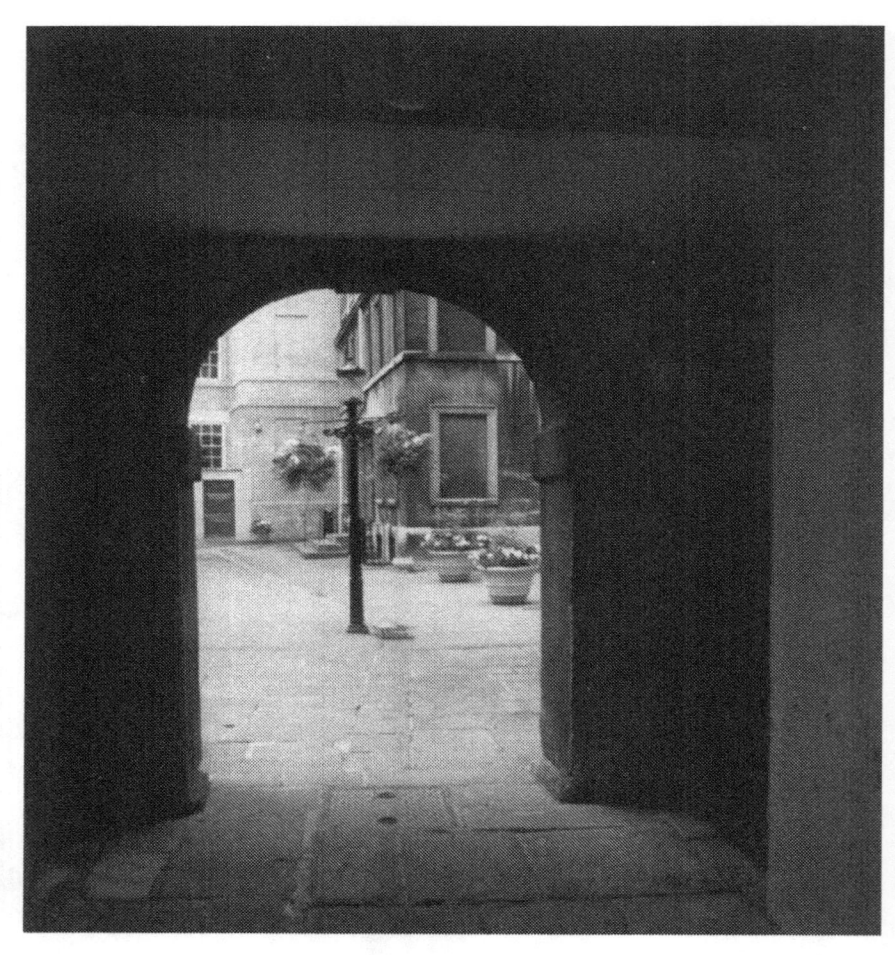

Old Doorway: Bath, England, 1984.

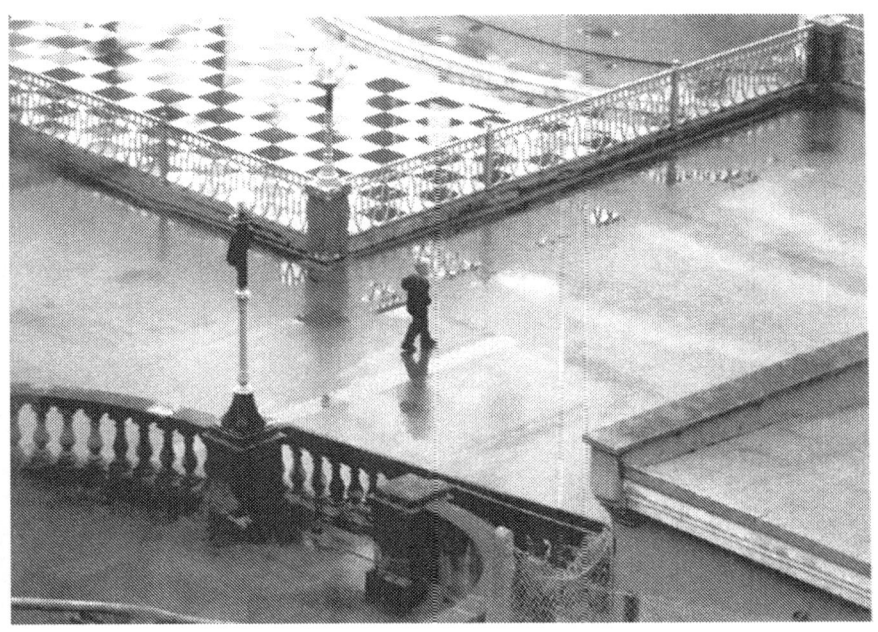

"Adam At The Crossroads of Life," Scarborough, Yorkshire, 2001. The young man appears to be walking across a gigantic game board. My hope is he'll be more than a pawn there...

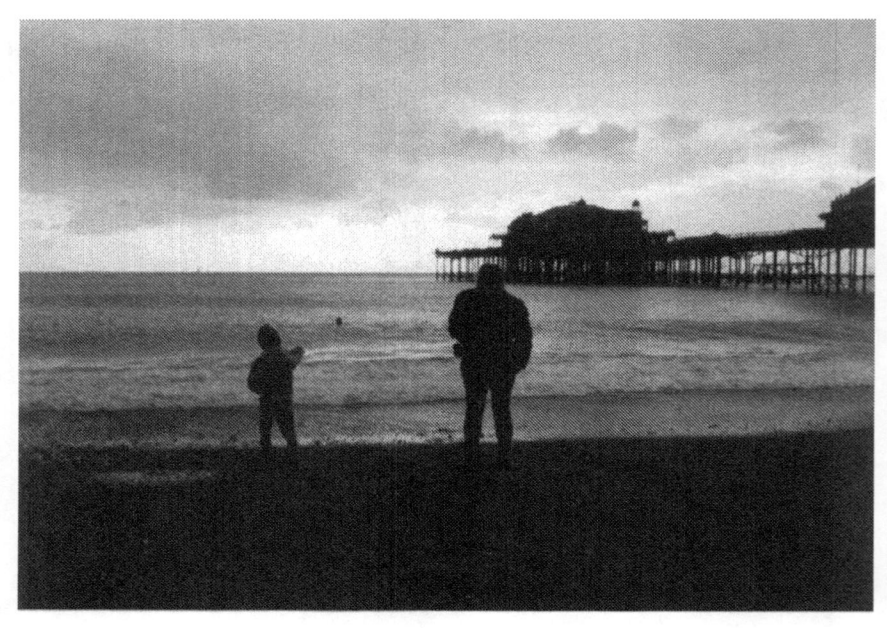

"Skipping Stones by Old Brighton Pier," UK 2001

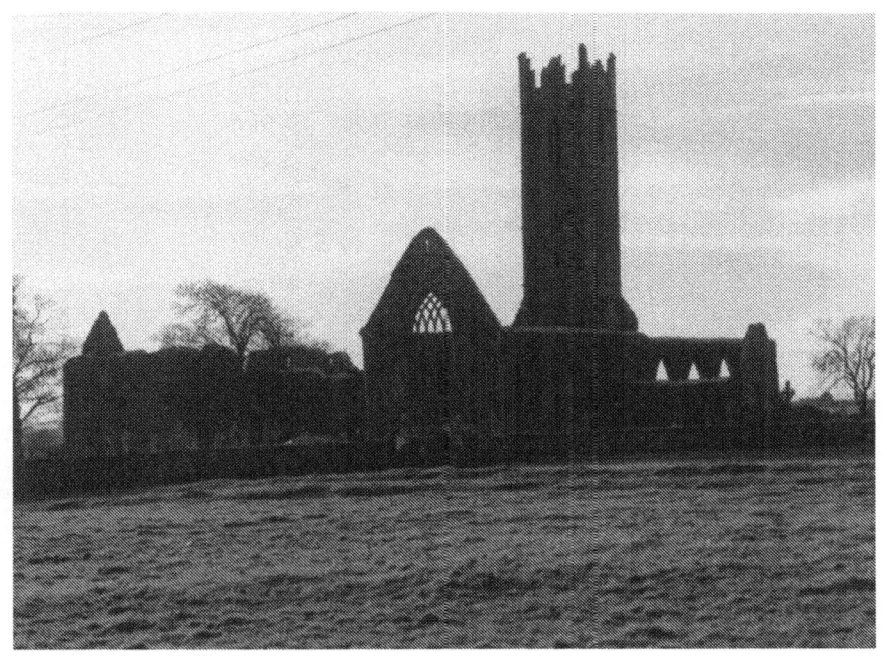

Burned Monastery; Rural Ireland, 1999.
I was constantly coming upon such sights, as if stage sets for a forgotten tragedy – but of course the tragedy has *not* been forgotten...

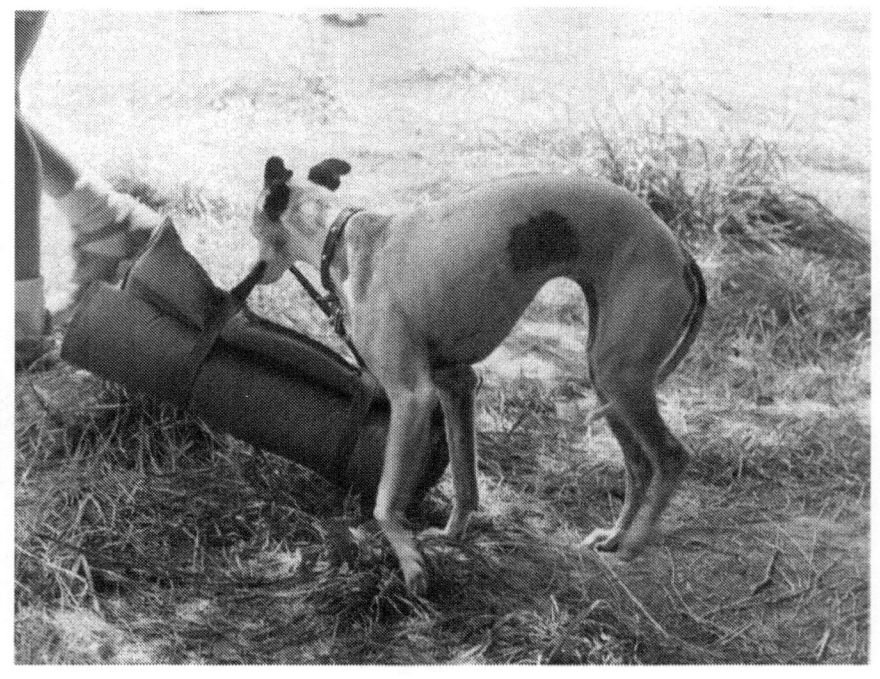

Annie the Whippet, A rescue dog, she followed her new master everywhere, never leaving her side. She carried her own bed... Rural Missouri, 1987.

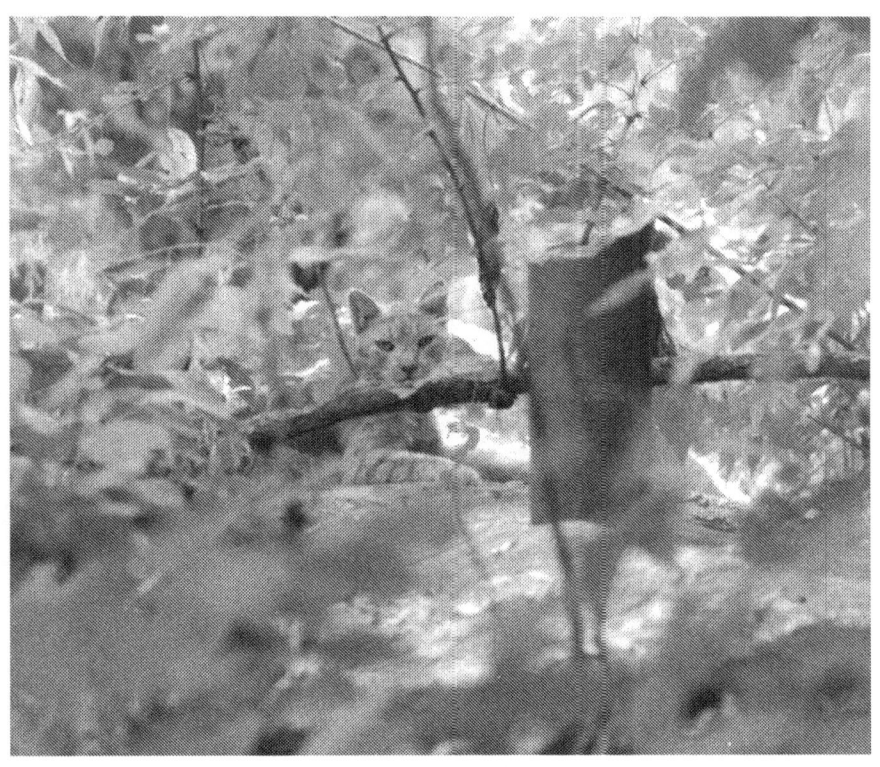

"You Can't See Me," Middle Grove, Missouri, 2000.

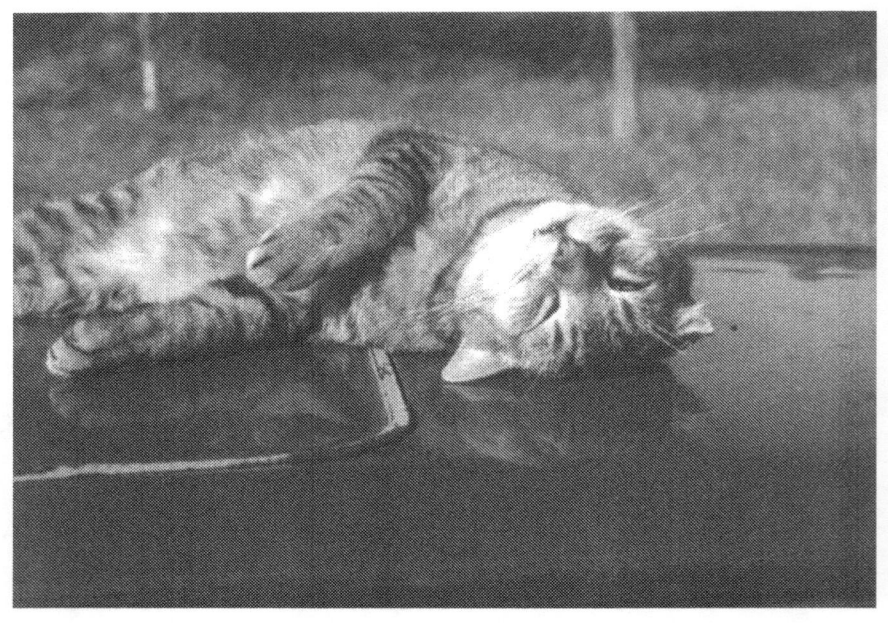

"A Different View," Middle Grove, Missouri, 2006

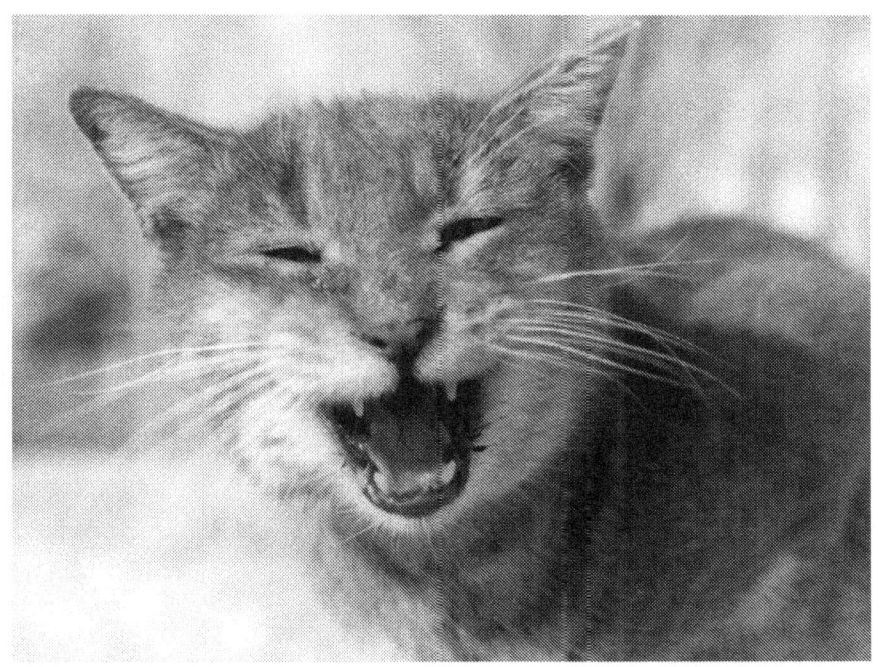

Feline Laughter, Middle Grove, Missouri, 2006

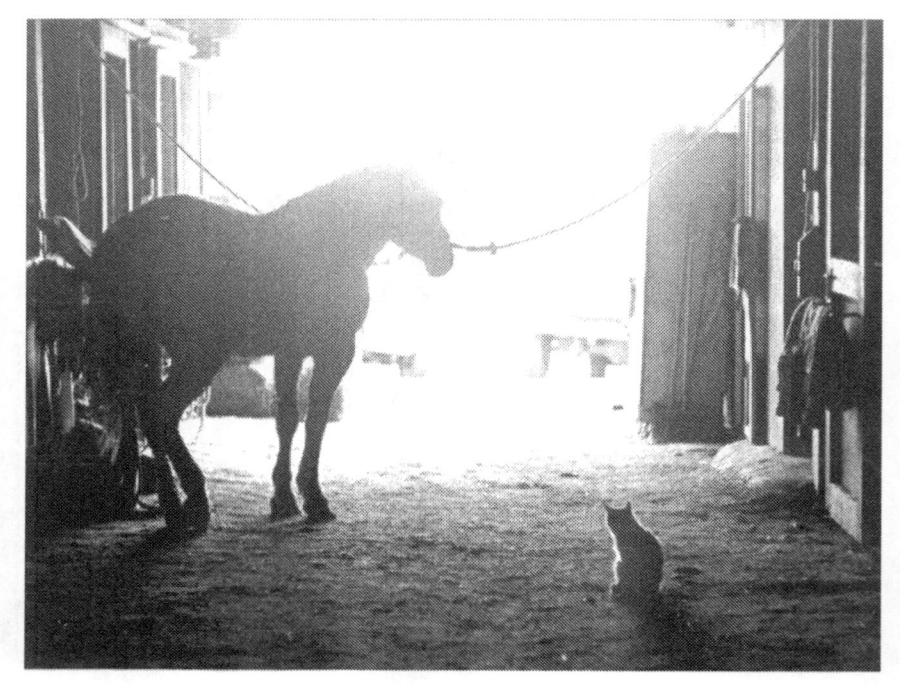

Barn Friends; Callaway County, Missouri, 1992

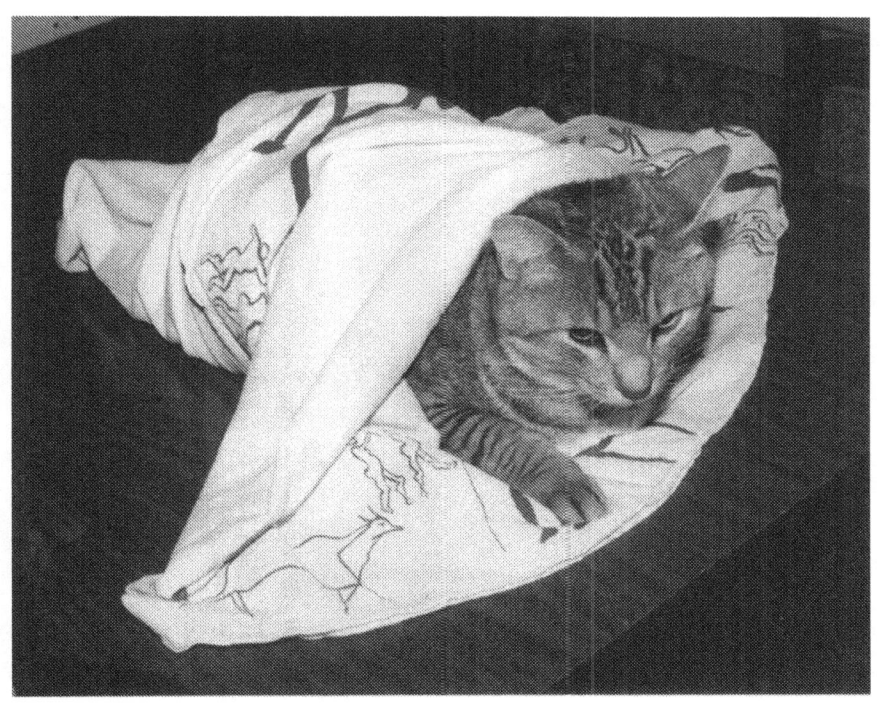

"All Wrapped Up," Middle Grove, Missouri, 1999.
Yes, the cat did it by himself!

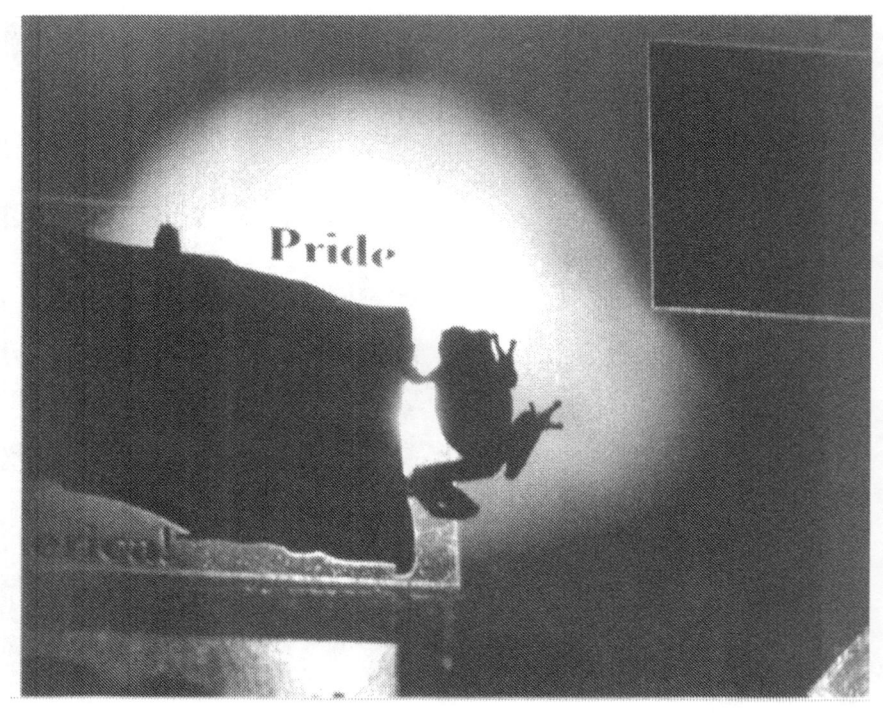

"Proud To Be A Frog." Columbia, Missouri, 1992.
One of my favorites, and a complete accident. Maybe part of being a
photographer is achieving some awareness of those accidents?

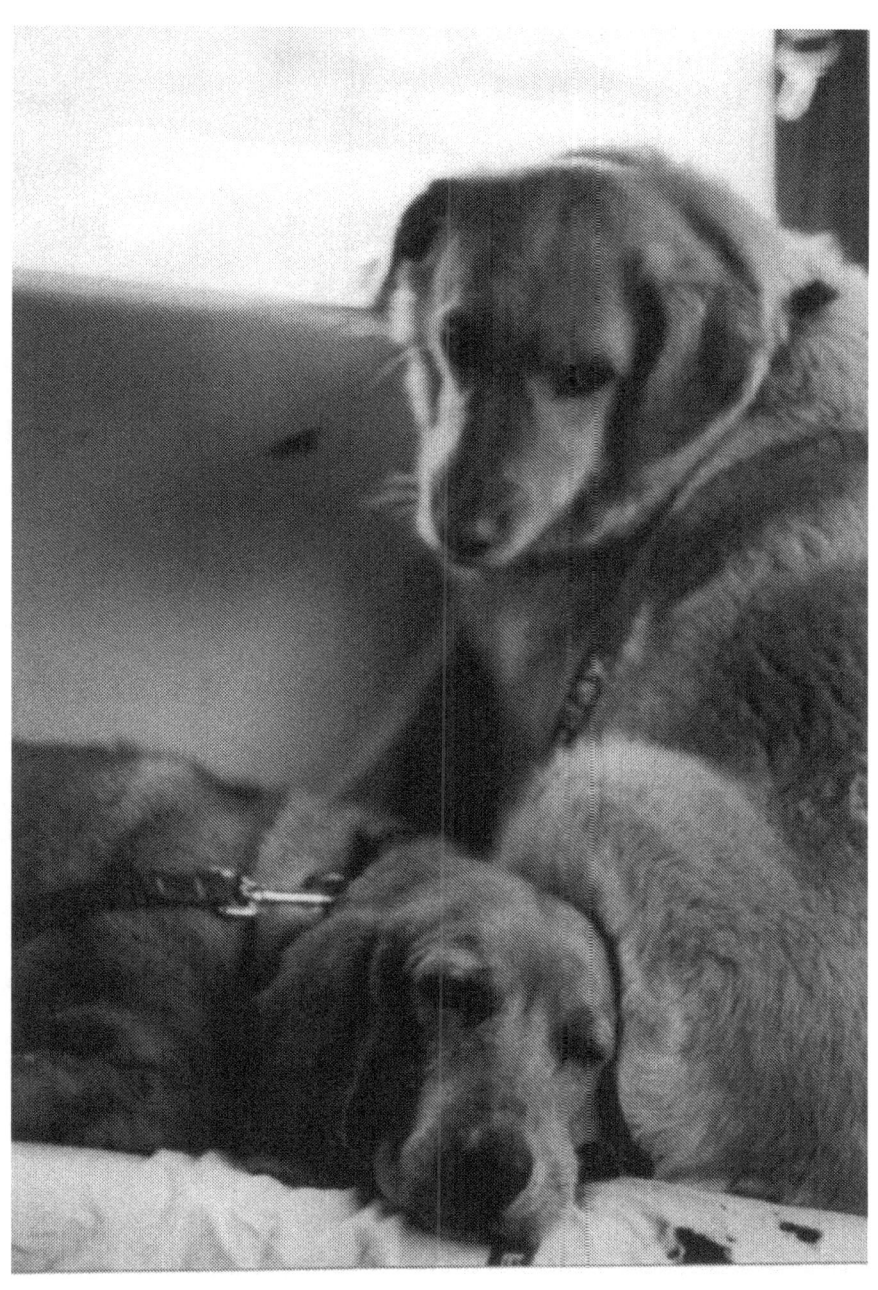

'Two Dogs; One Seat," Middle Grove, Missouri, 2000

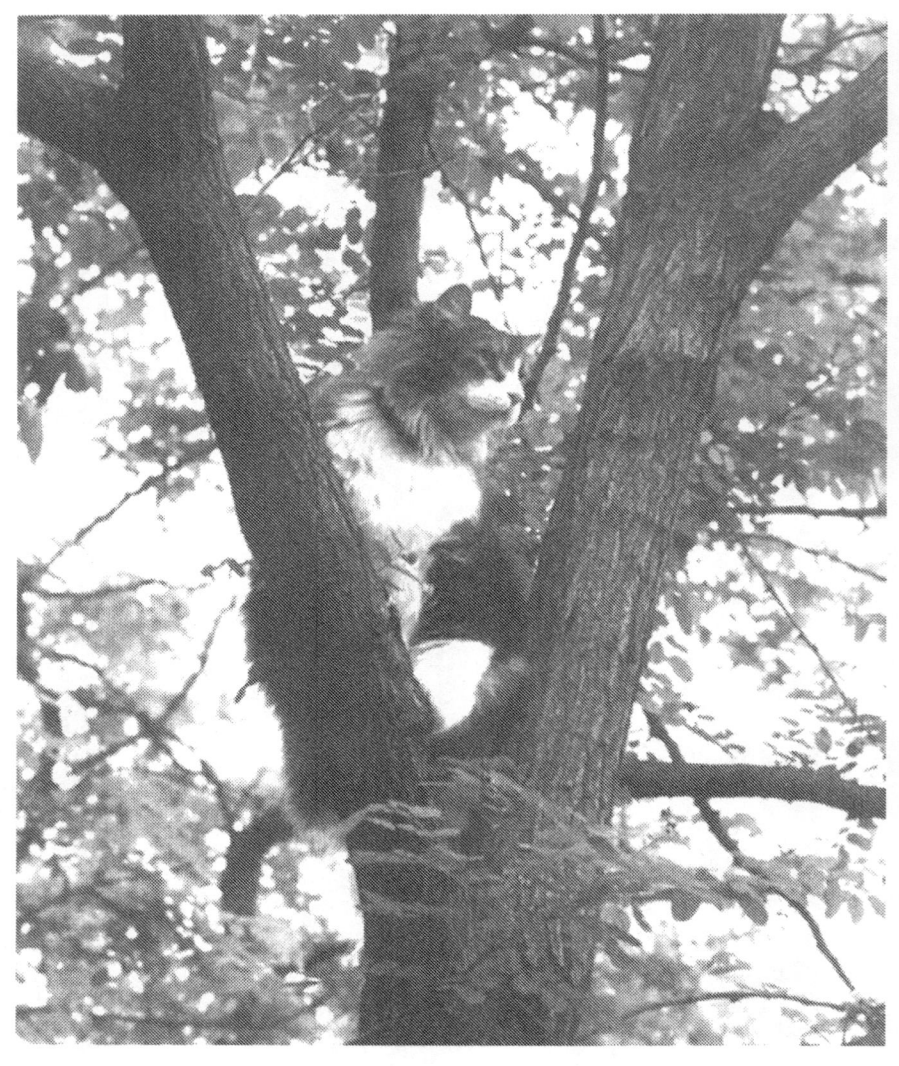

"Beast of Prey," Middle Grove, Missouri, 2001

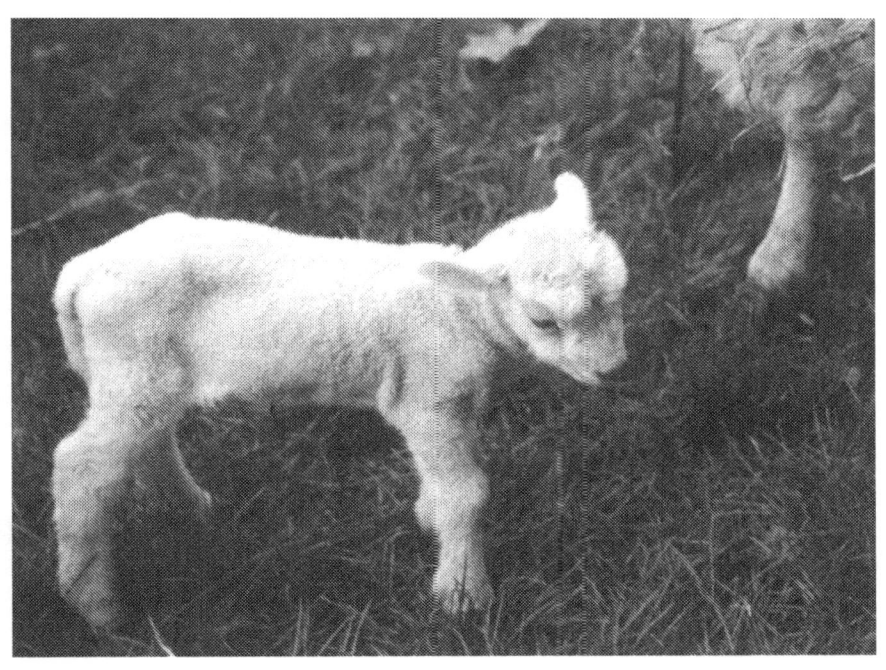

Newborn Innocent, Yorkshire, UK, 2002

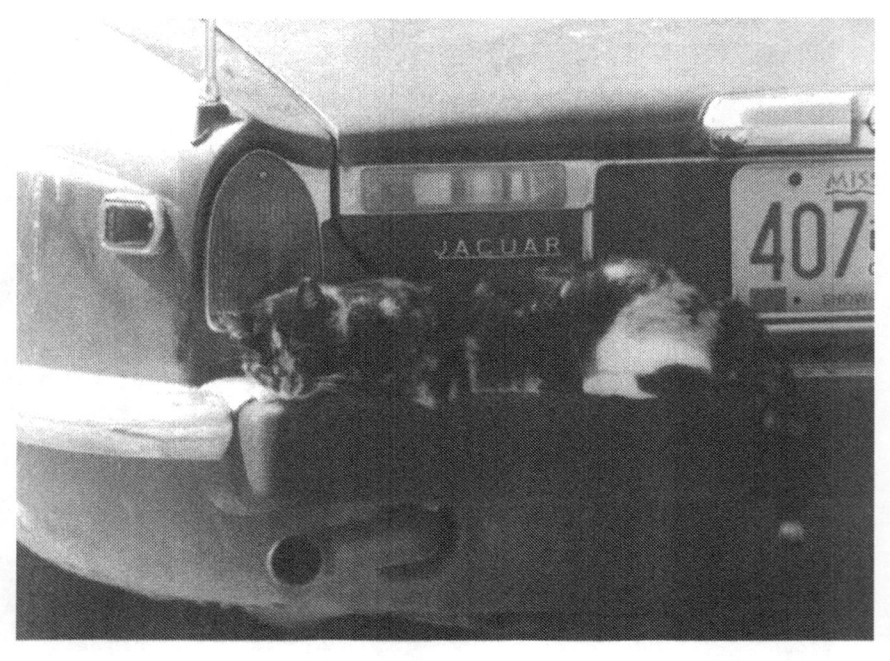

"When I Grow Up," Middle Grove, Missouri, 2006.

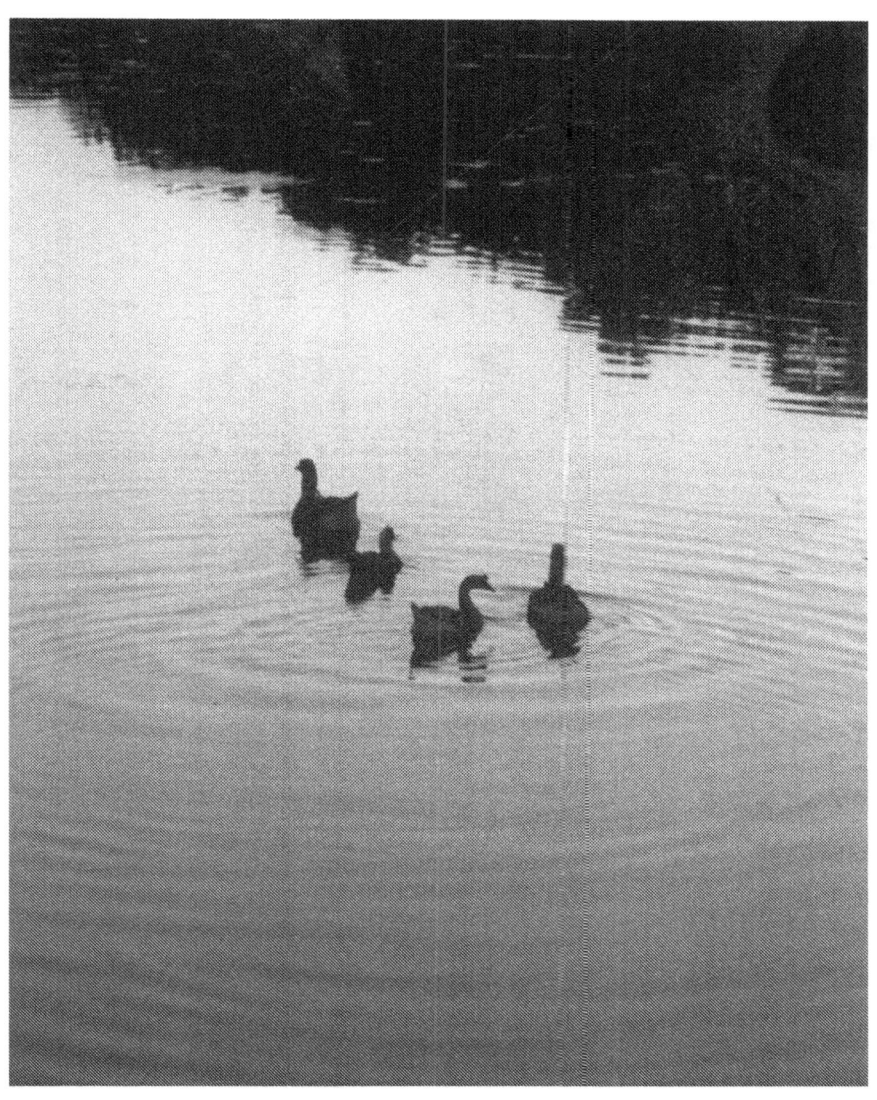

Evening Ducks, Moberly, Missouri, 2000

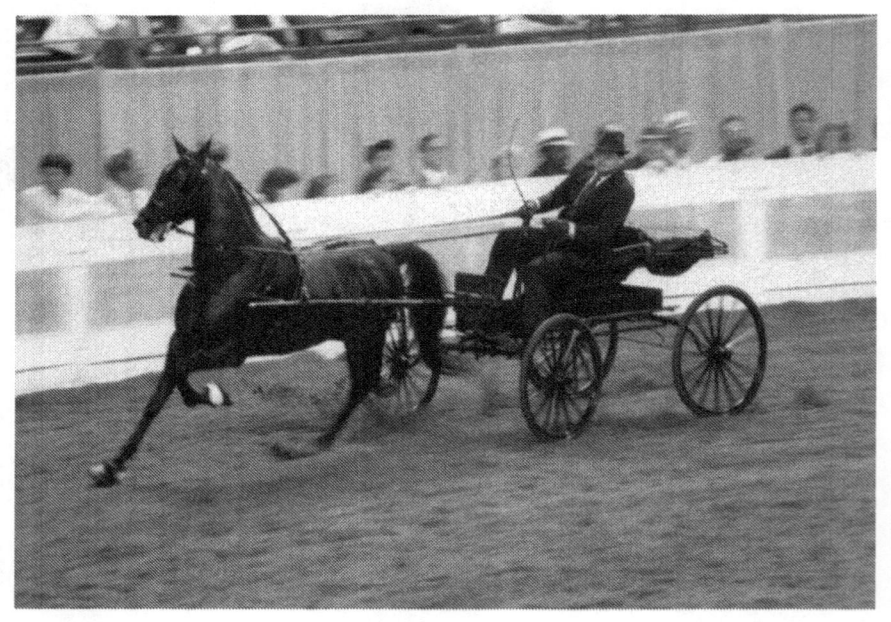

Louisville, Kentucky, Saddlebred World Championship, 1989

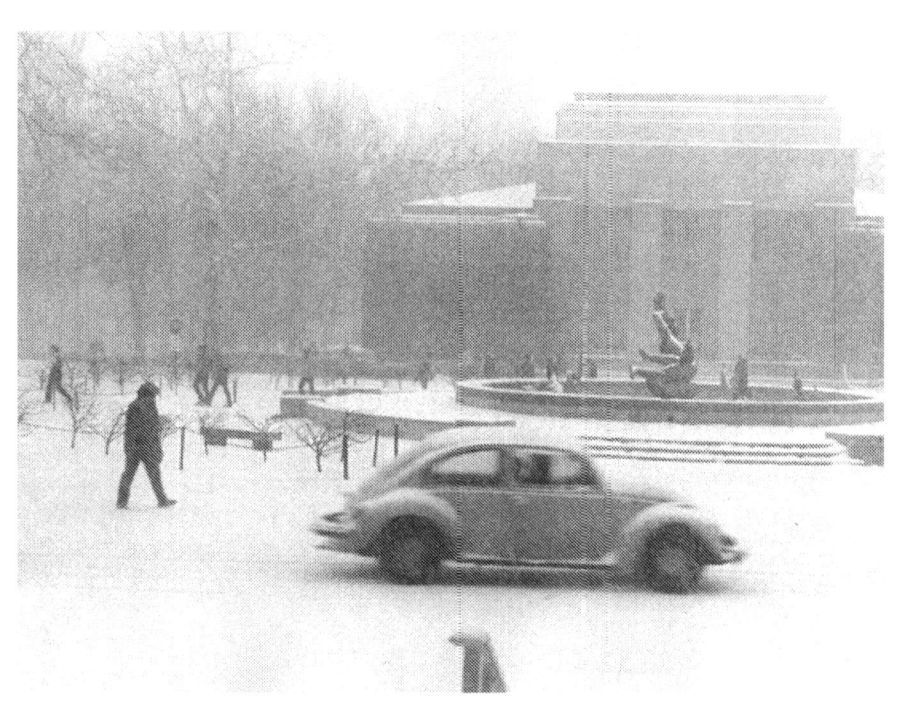

Snow Flurries, Indiana U, Bloomington, 1985

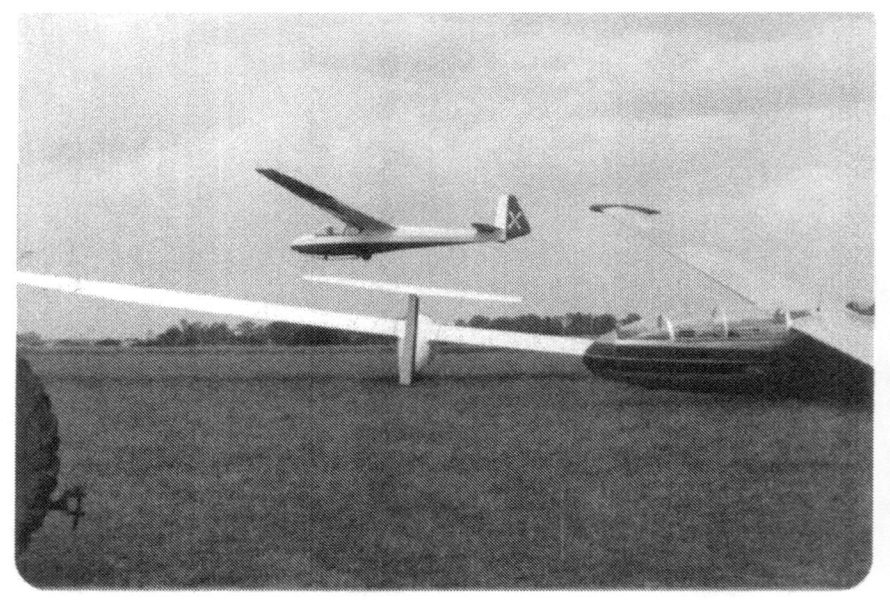

Gliding Club, near Shalebourne, Wiltshire, UK, 1984

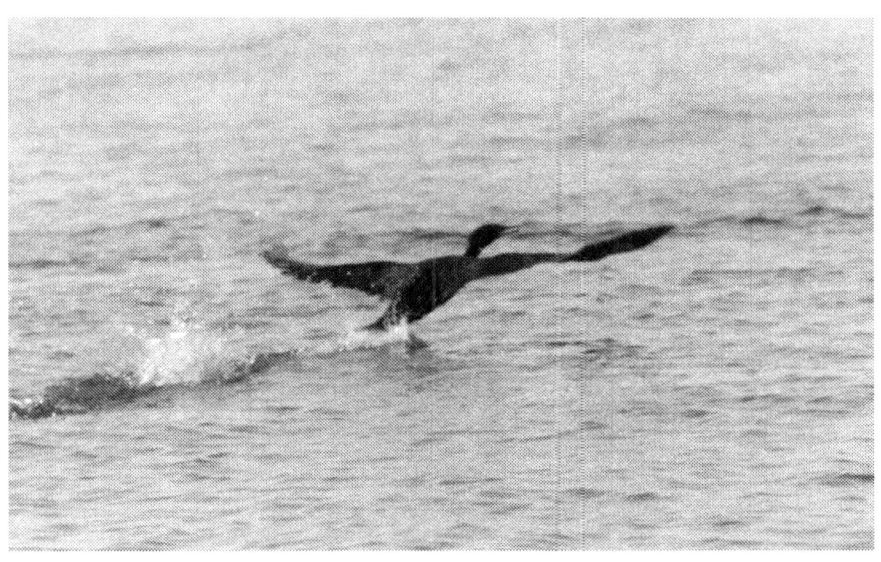

Cormorant, Near Fort Frances, Ontario, Canada, 2006

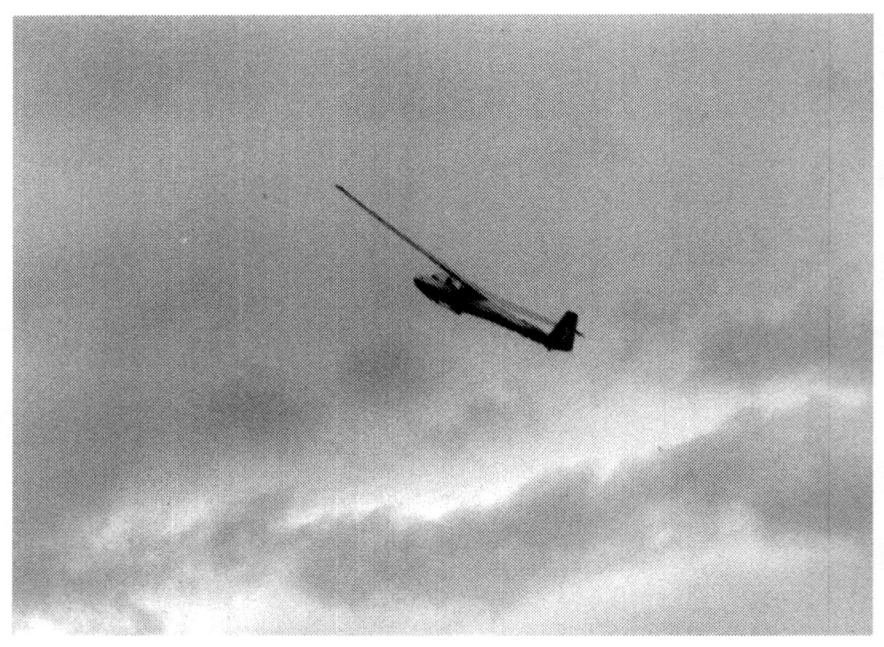

Sailplane; Shalebourne, England, 1987

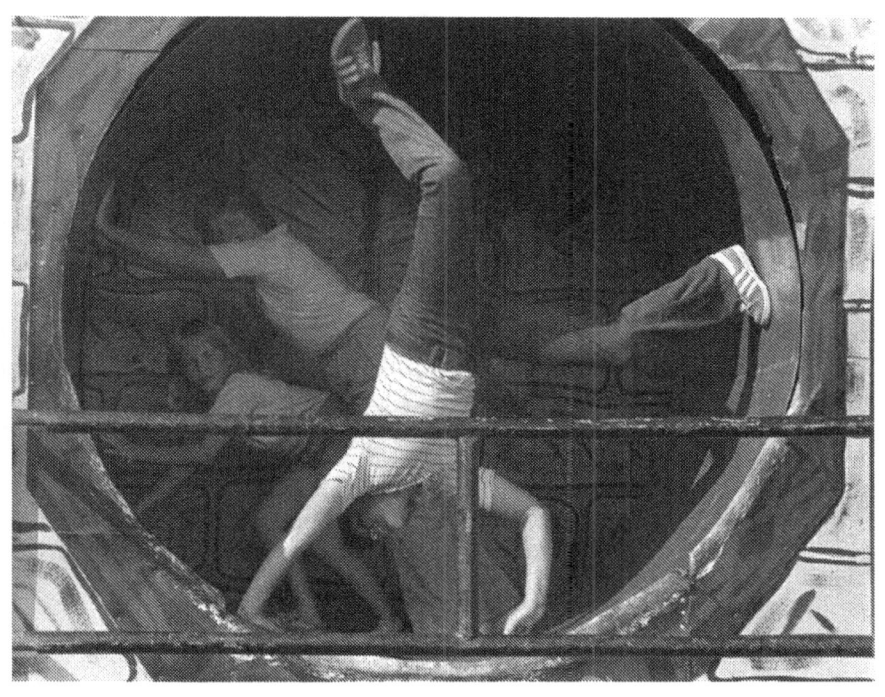

"In The Great Wheel," Norfolk, Virginia, 1982.

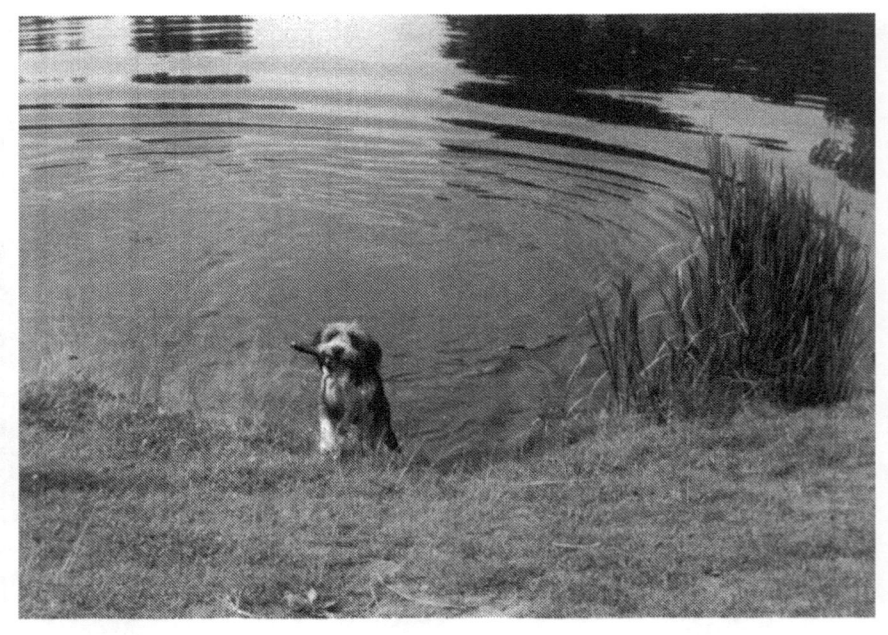

Wet Dog, York, England, 2002

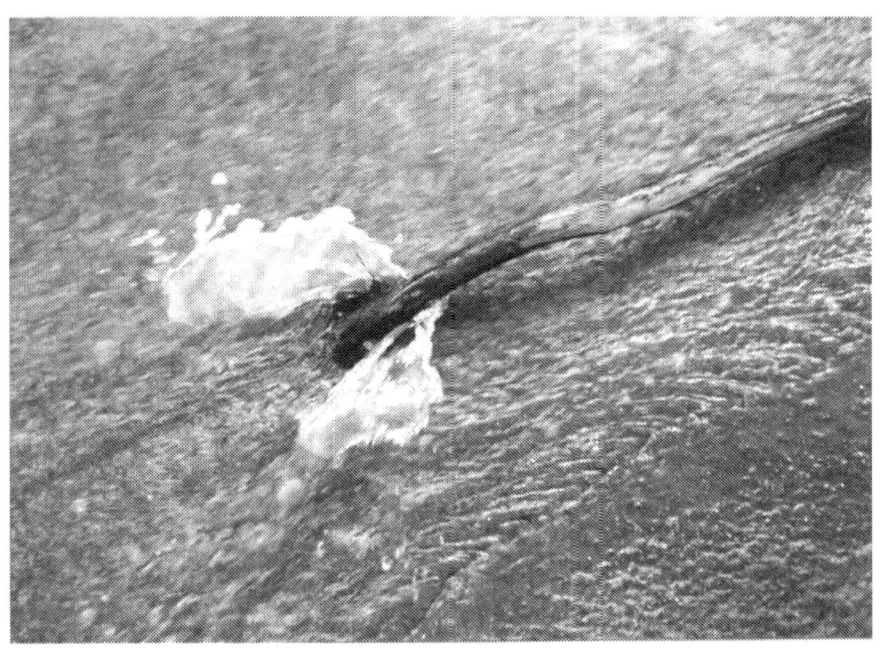

"Like a Twig in a Fast-Moving Stream," Moberly, Missouri, 2002

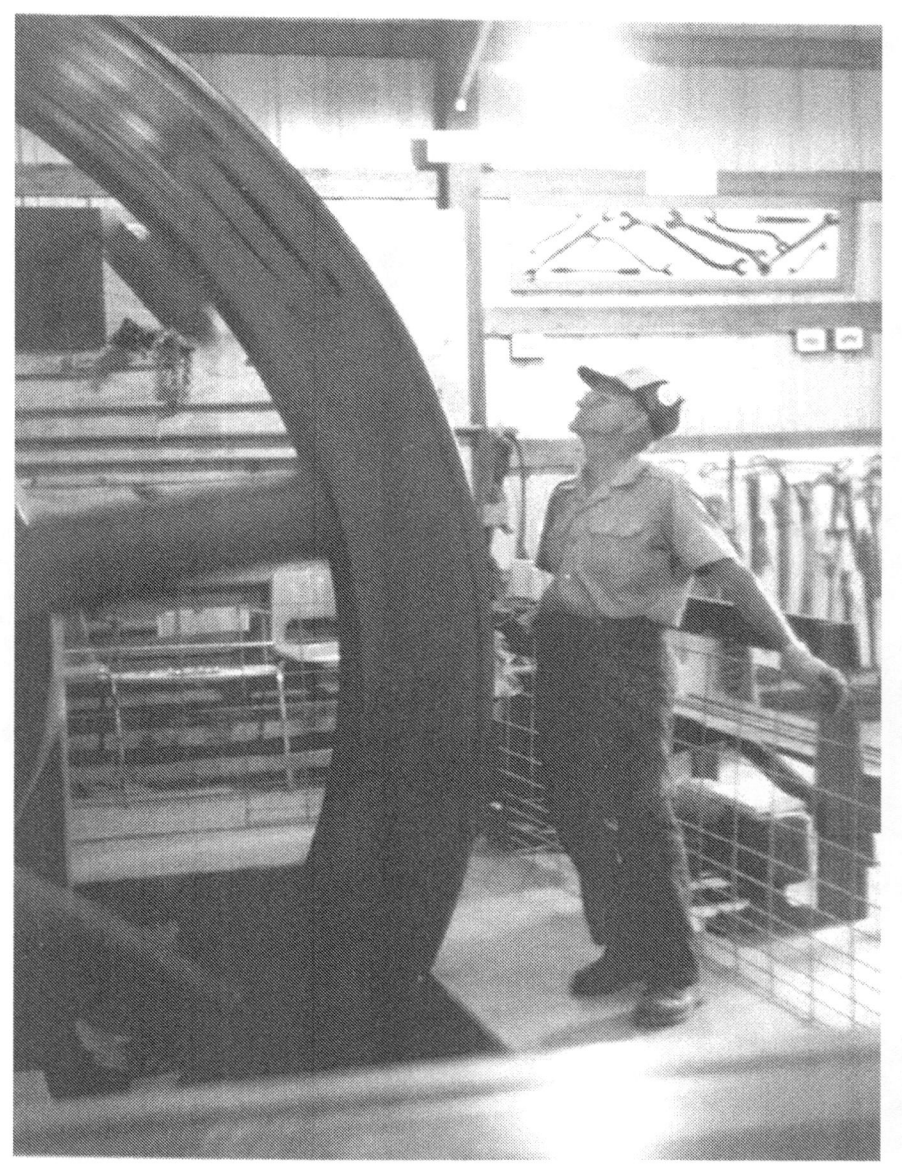

"Tending the Machine," Macon, Missouri, 2000

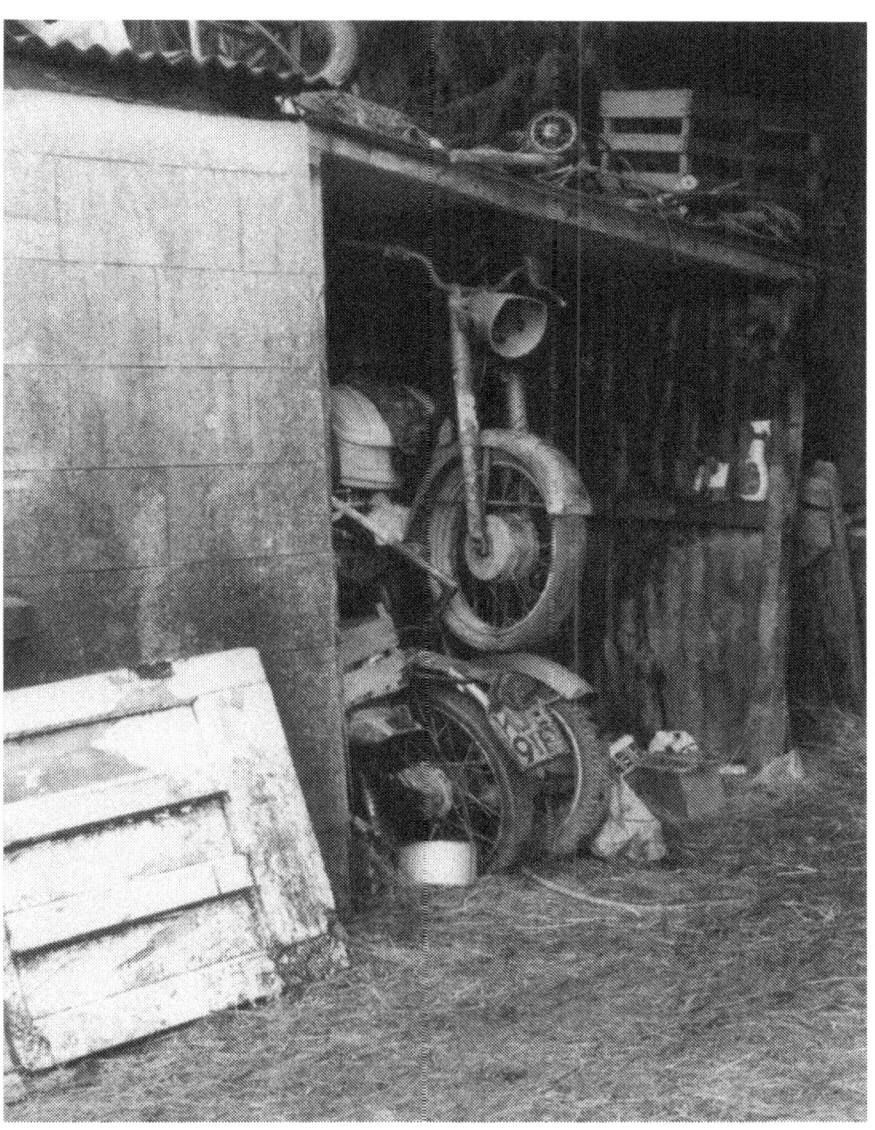

Old Motorbikes; Wales, UK, 1988

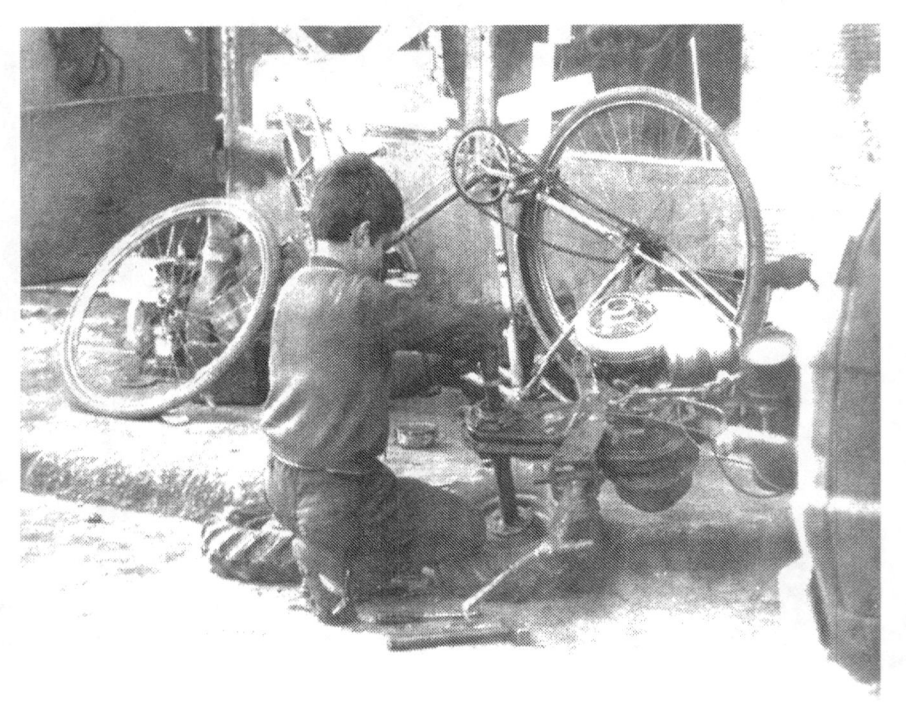

Boy Hard At Work; Chania, Crete, 1981.

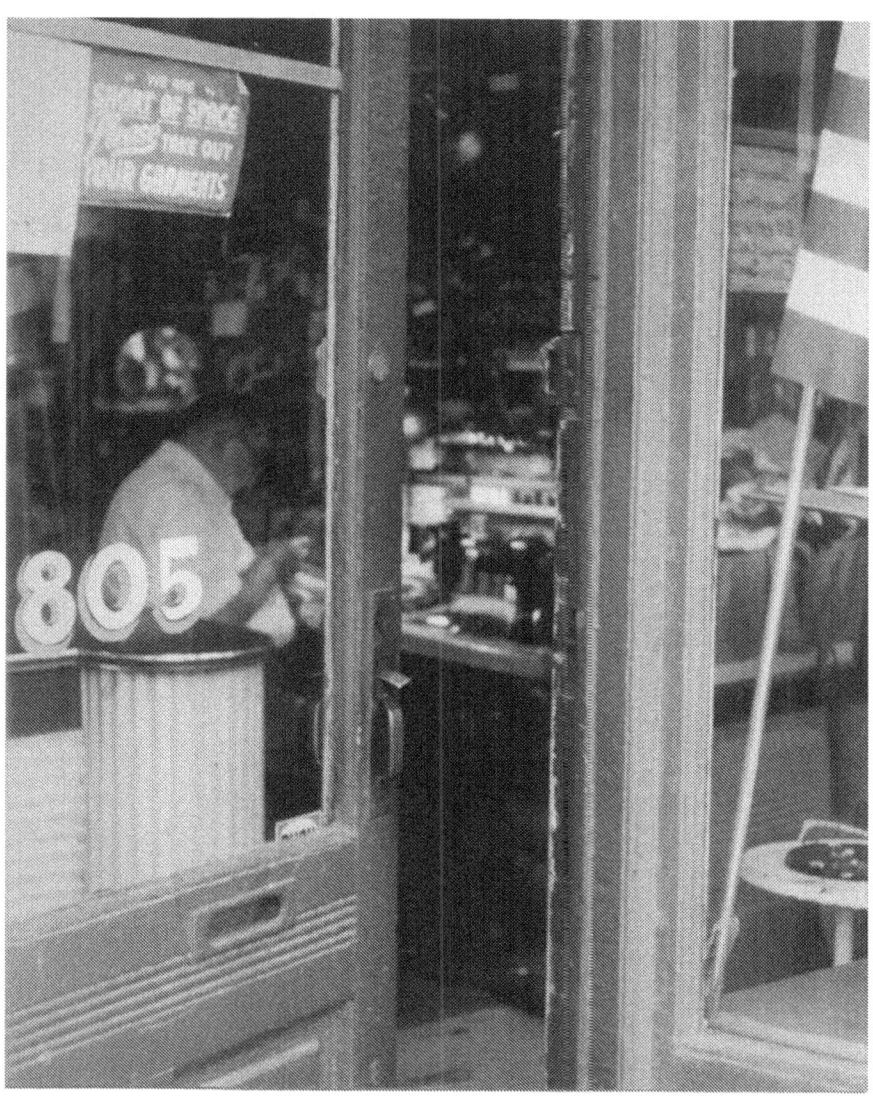

Tailor; Cincinnati, Ohio, 1973.

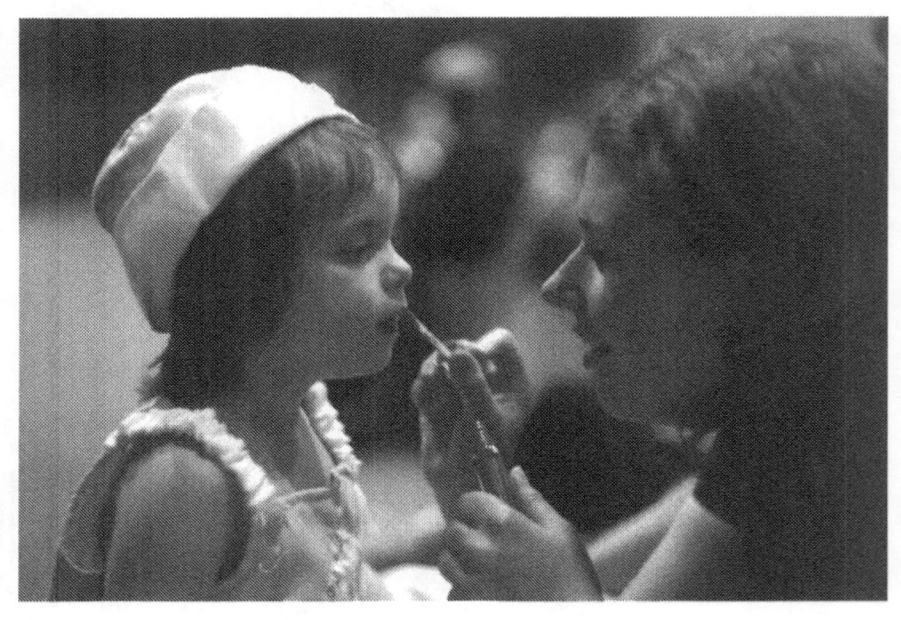

Getting Ready For The Big Night, Moberly, Missouri, 2005

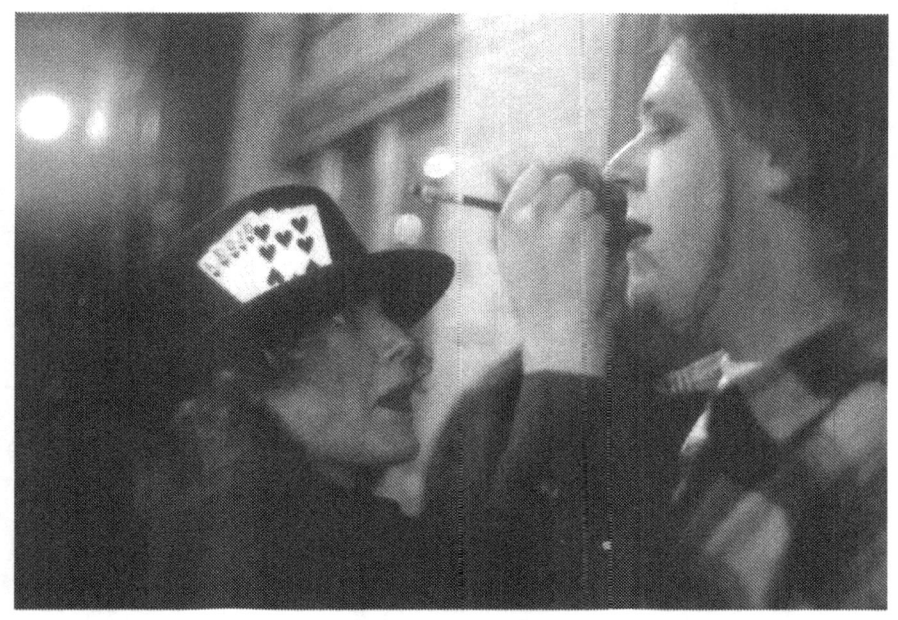

Halloween Street Party; Columbia, Misscuri, 2003

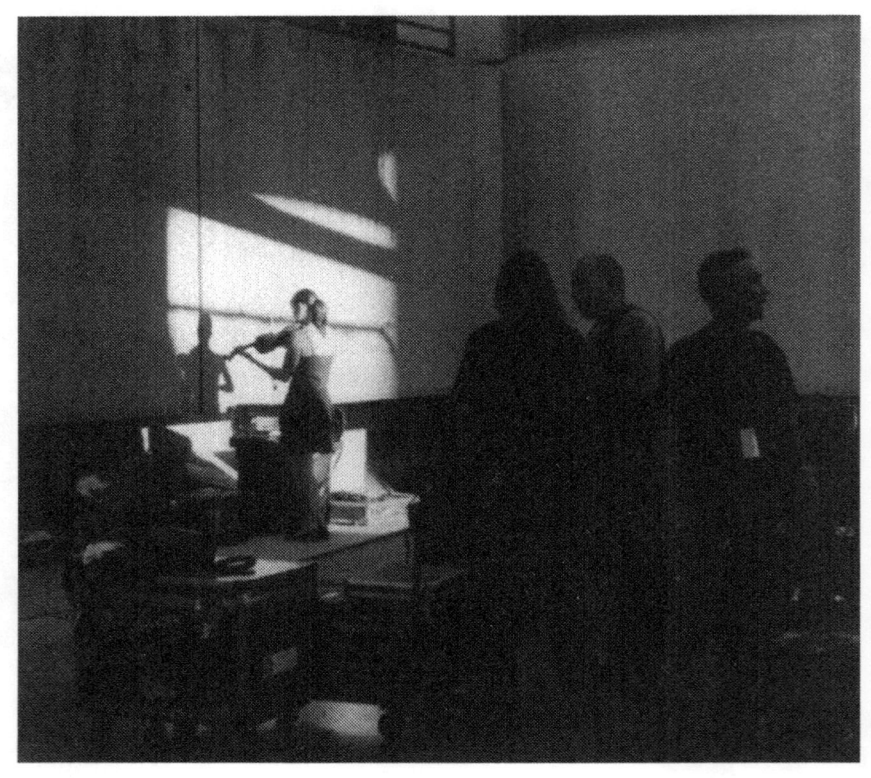

"Warming Up," Kansas City, Missouri, 2006
You should have seen this one! Classical violinist follows Irish Punk
band at local Irish Festival. There she was in her evening dress, alone in the
darkness, surrounded by terrifying hardboys,,, when a ray of sun illuminated
her, and she began to play. Still, she faced the wall, and did not turn around
until her time to go on stage...

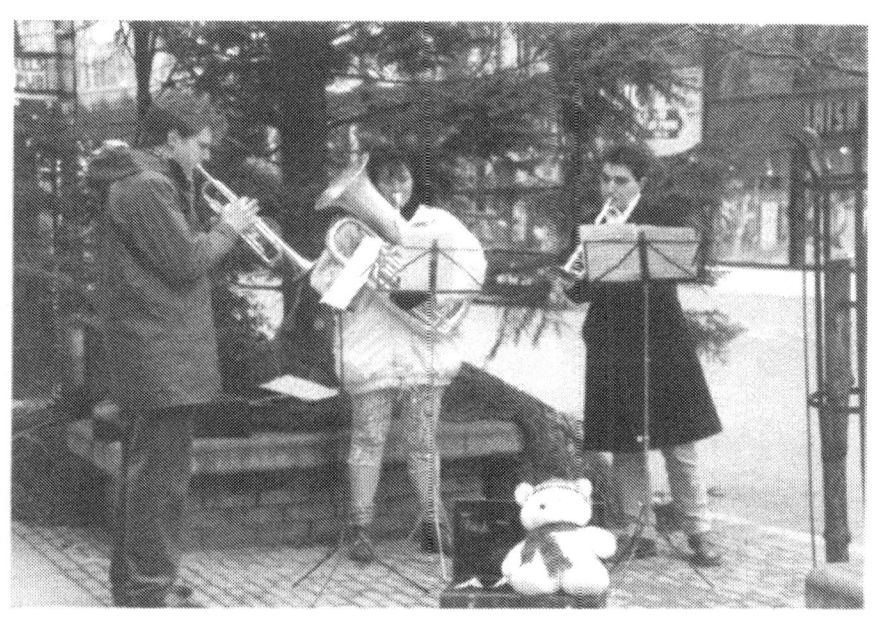

Street Band; Sligo, Ireland, 1989

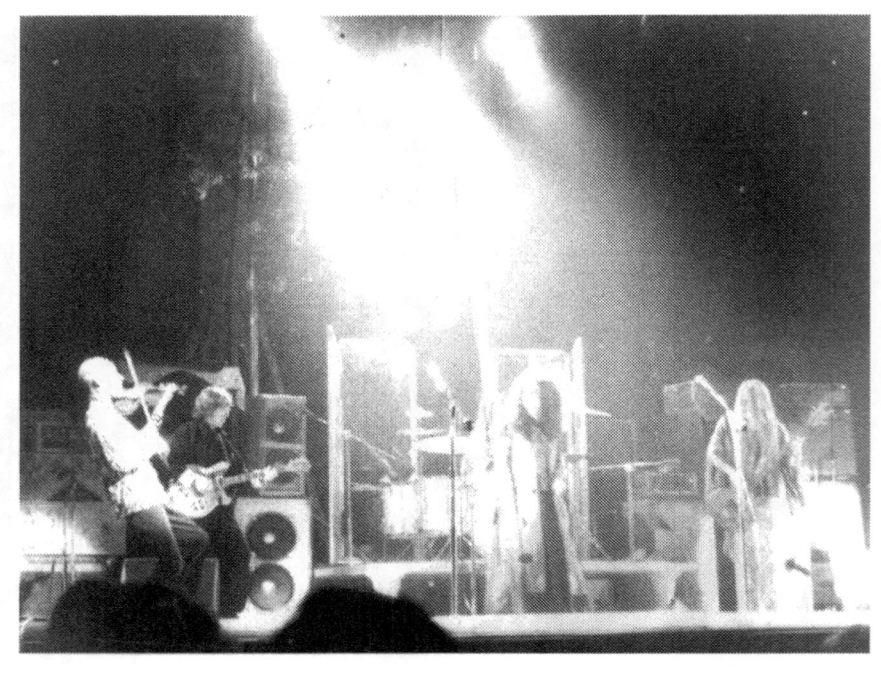

Very Early Jefferson Starship In Action; Cincinnati, Ohio, 1973

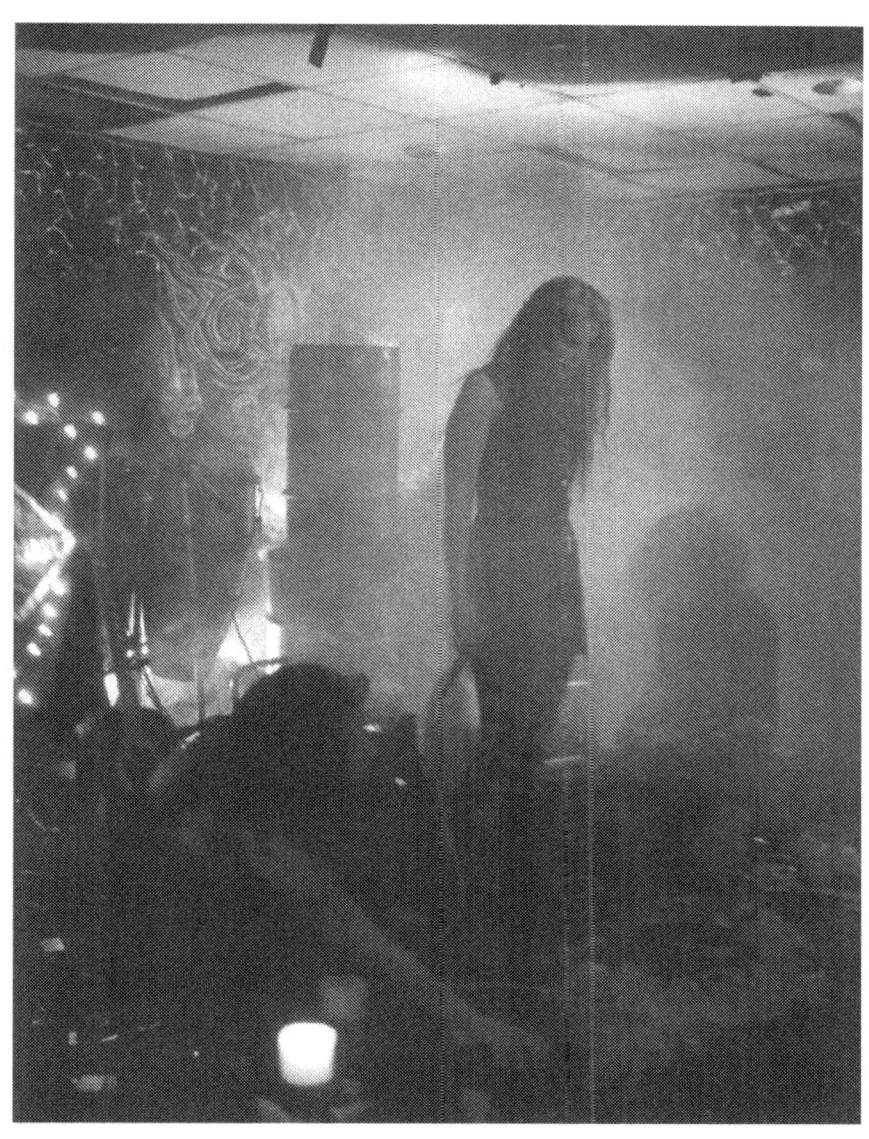

In Concert; Columbia, Missouri, 2000

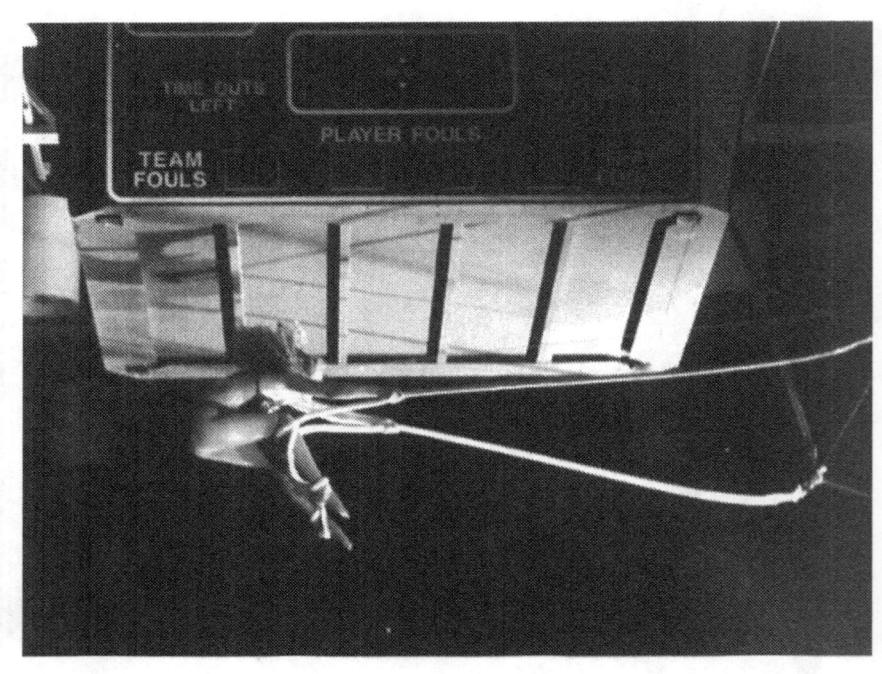

A High Degree Of Risk; Moberly, Missouri, 2006.

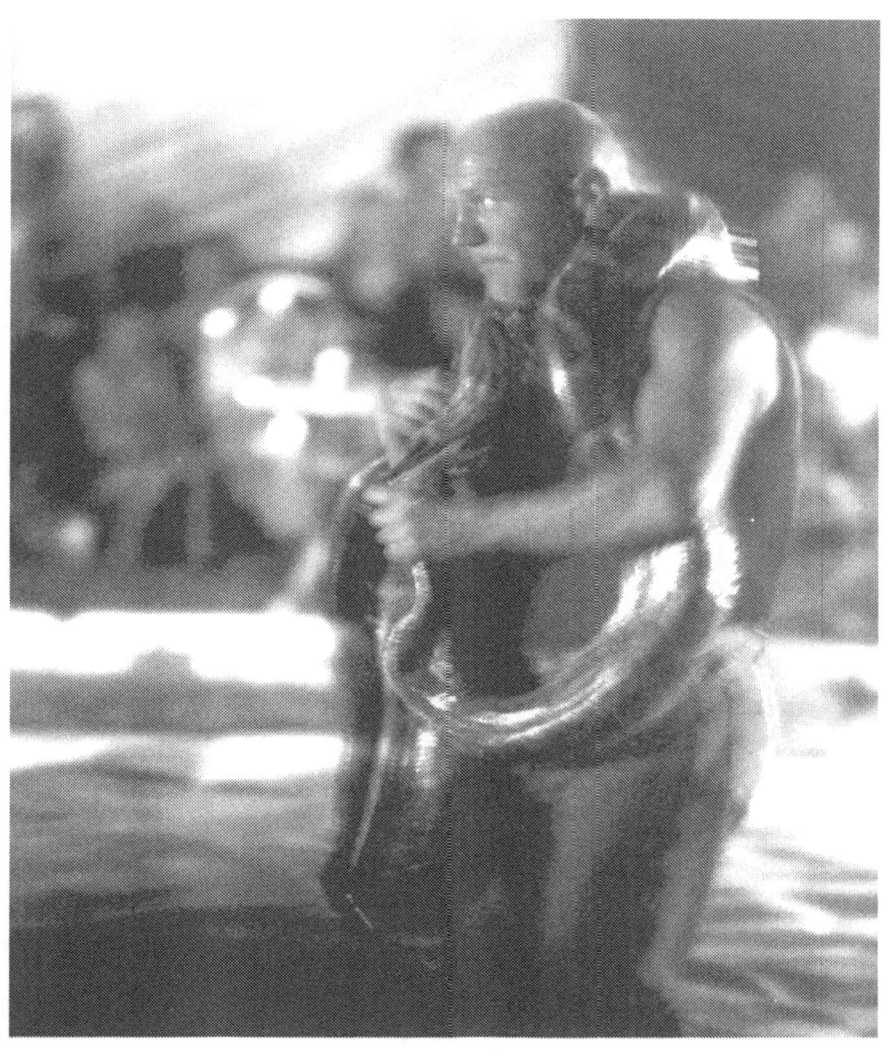

Circus Performer With Snake, Moberly, Missouri, 2005

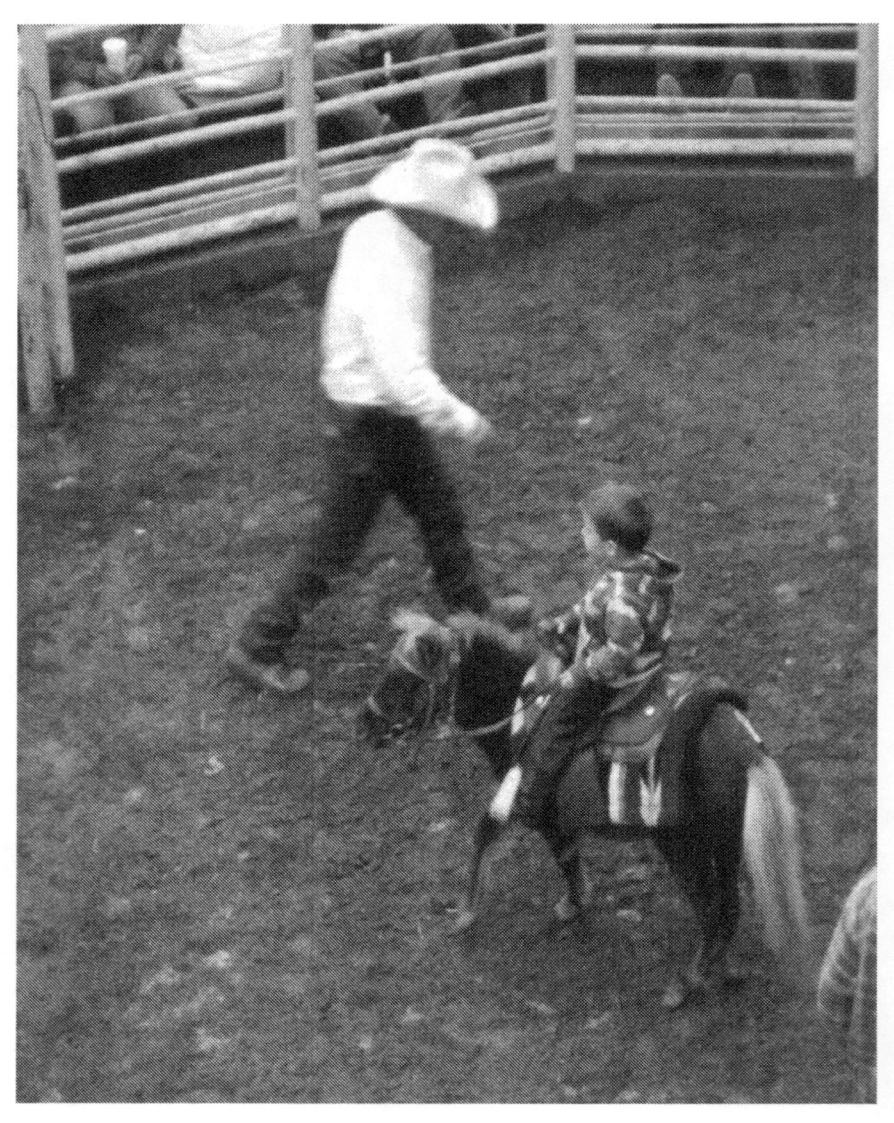

Very Young Rider, Mexico, Missouri, 2006

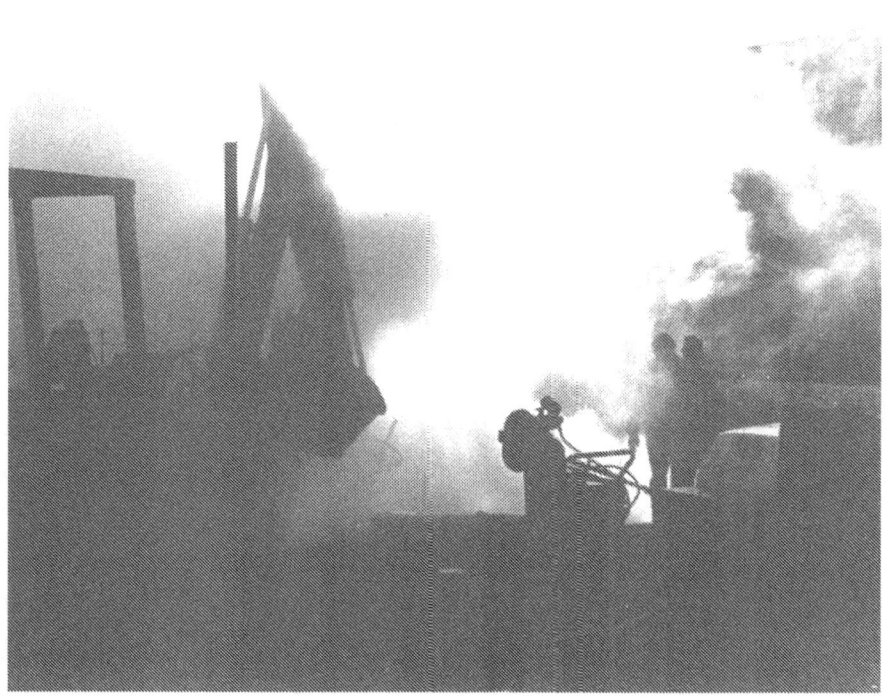

Broken Steam Jet Creates An Eerie Scene, Williamsburg, Virginia, 1982

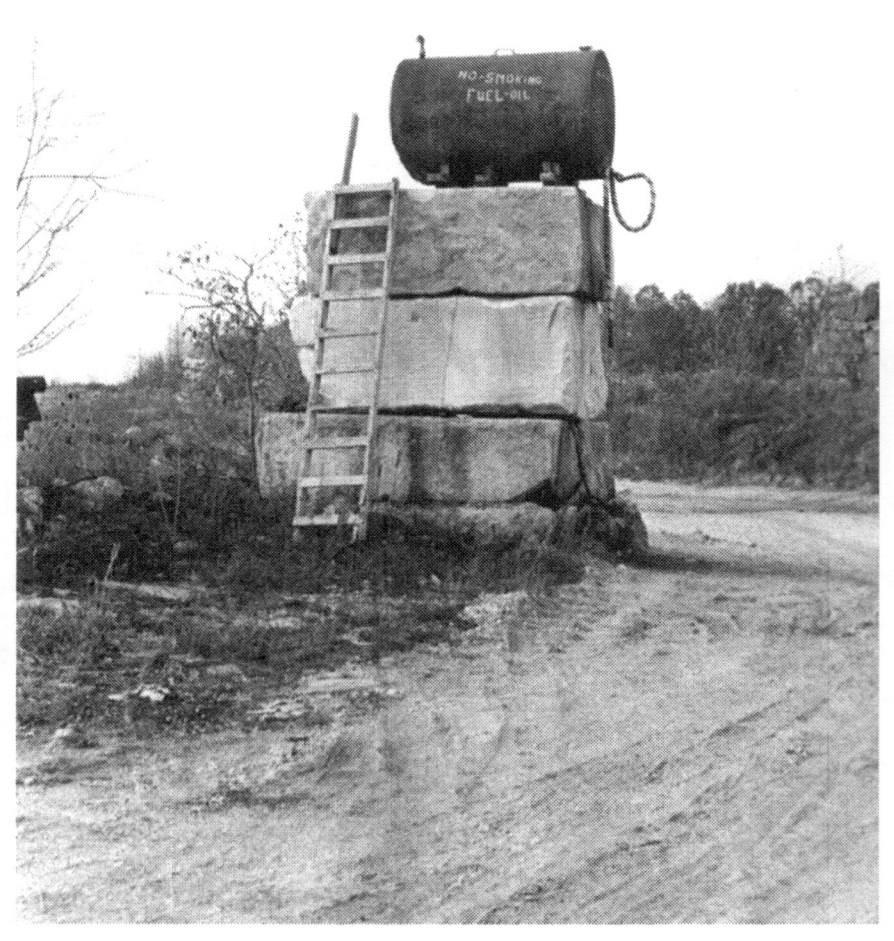

Stone Age Filling Station; Bloomington, Indiana, 1983

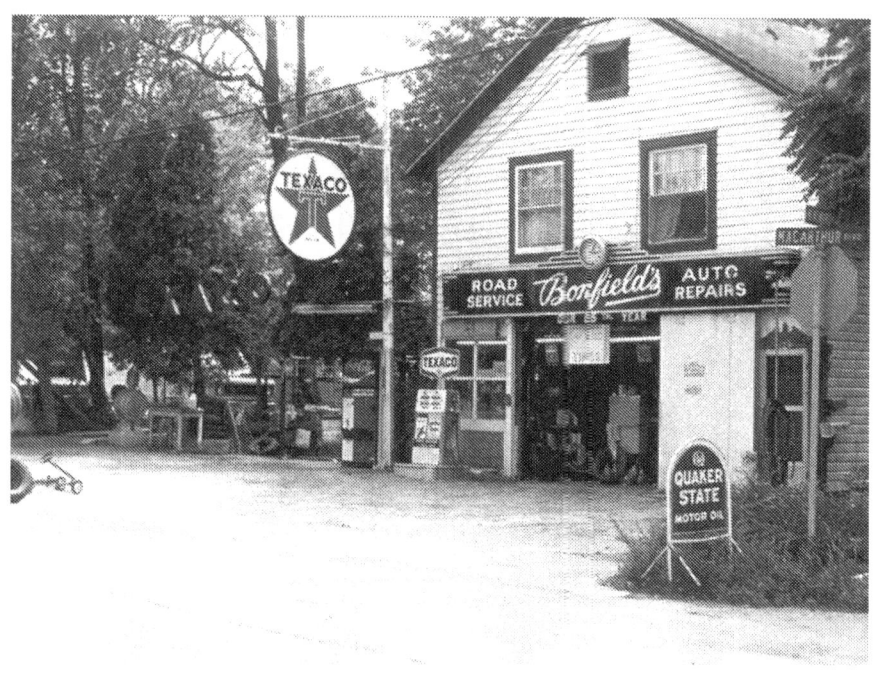

Very Old Gas Station; Washington DC, 1977

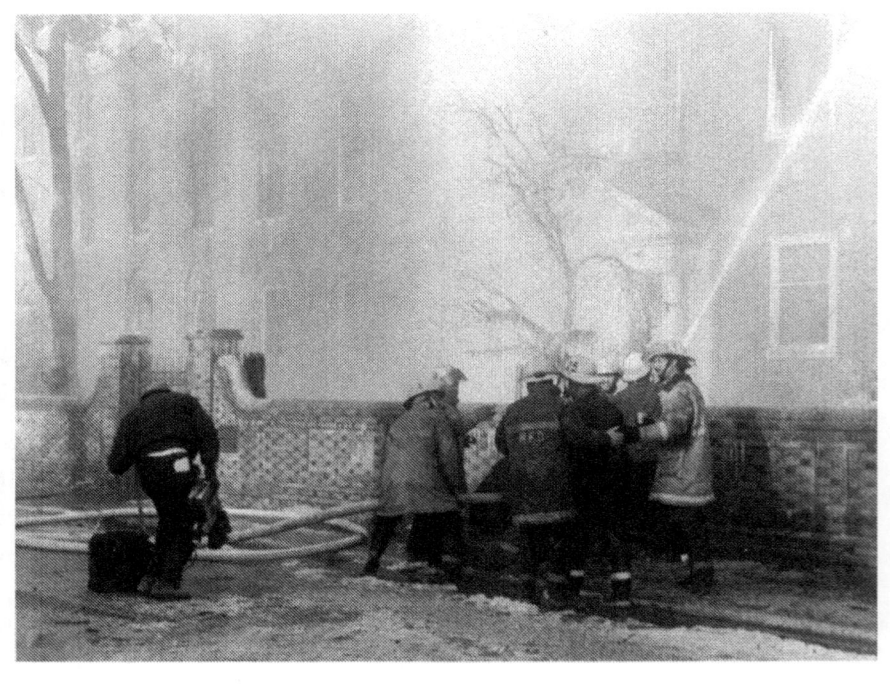

"Fire And Ice," College of William and Mary, Williamsburg, VA 1982

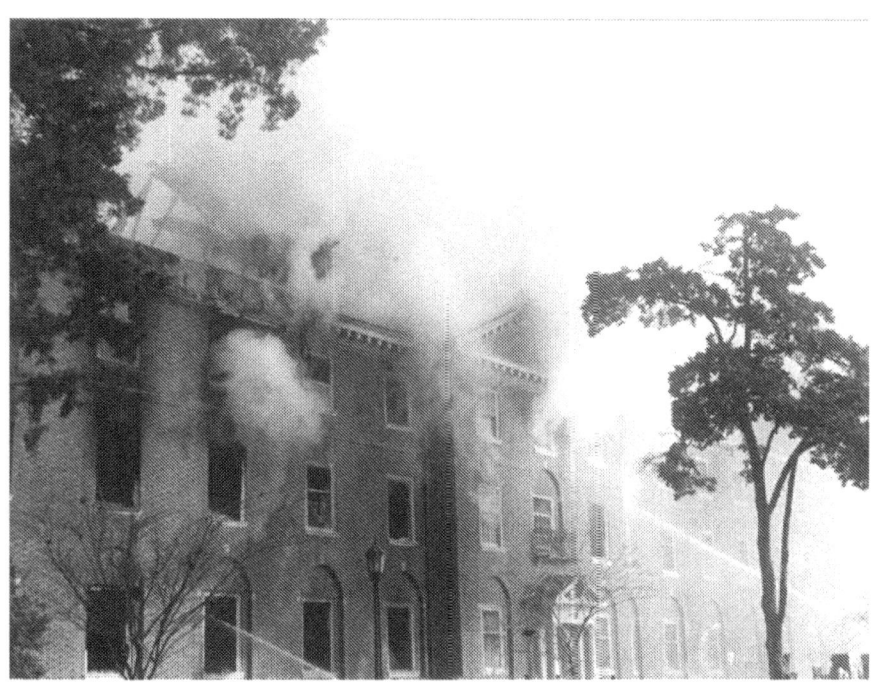

"Hottest Dorm On Campus" (same fire as previous), Williamsburg, Virginia, 1982

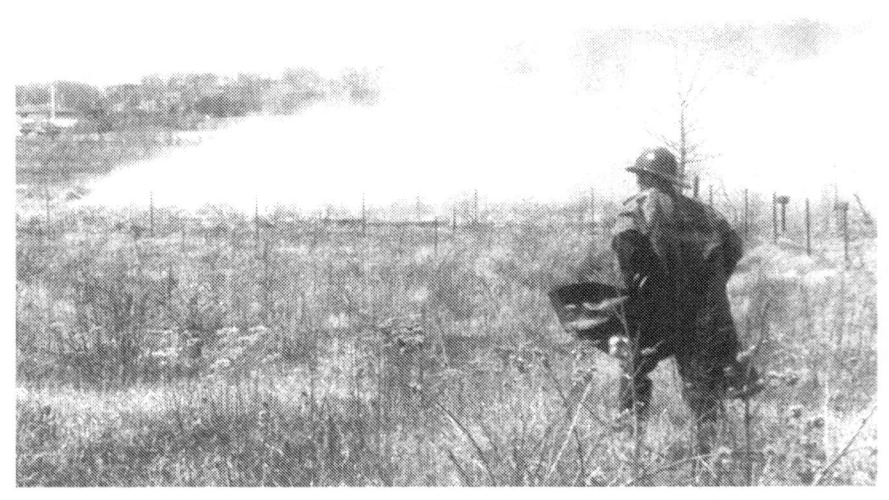

Fire Chief At Work; Rural Wisconsin, 1975

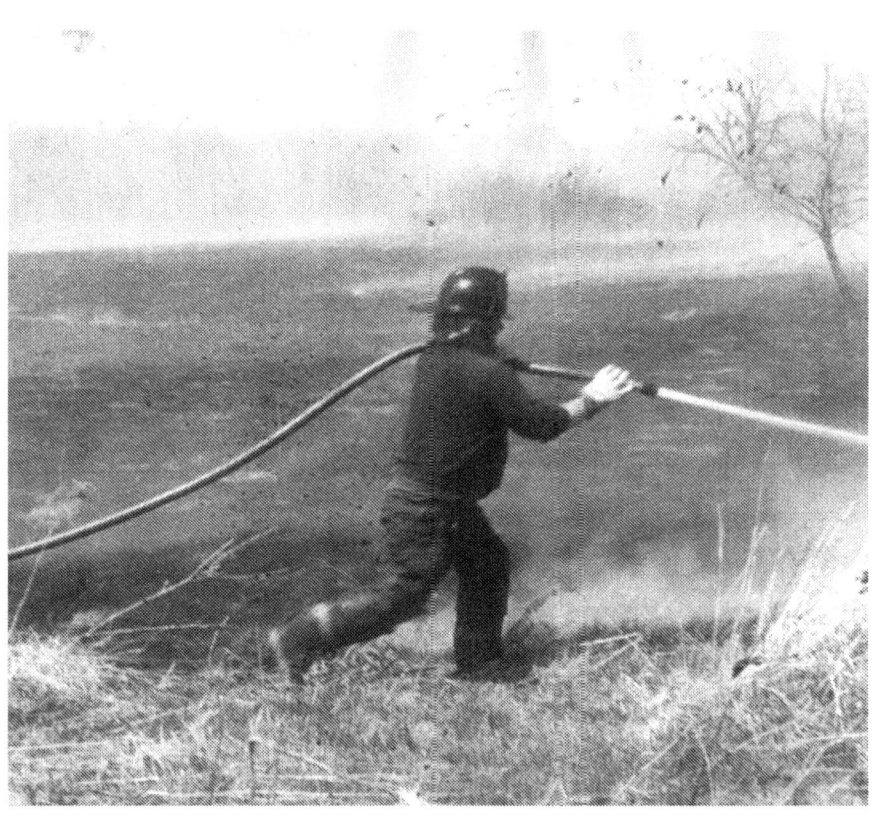

Volunteer Fireman; Rural Wisconsin, 1975

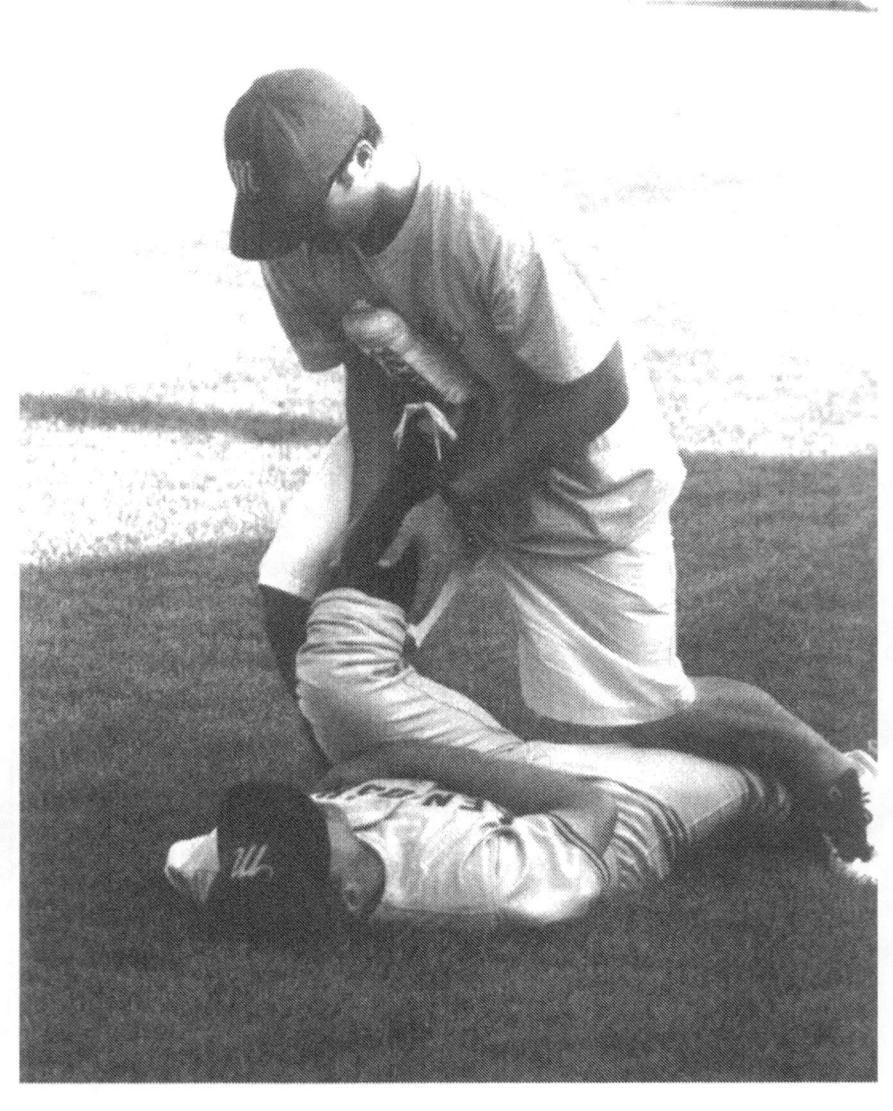

Pregame Stretches; Columbia, Missouri, 2004

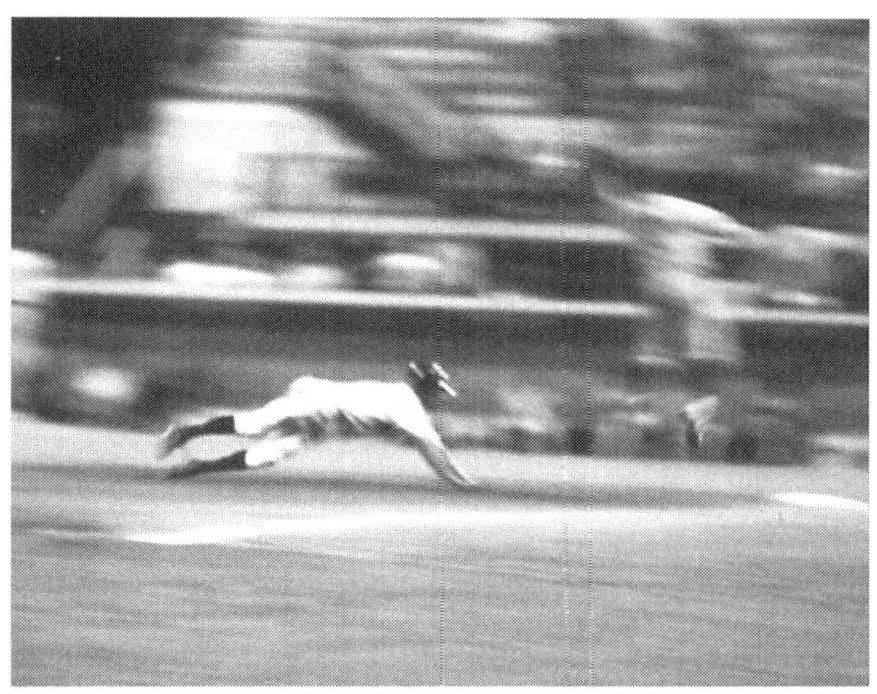

Sliding Into Home; Columbia, Missouri, 2004

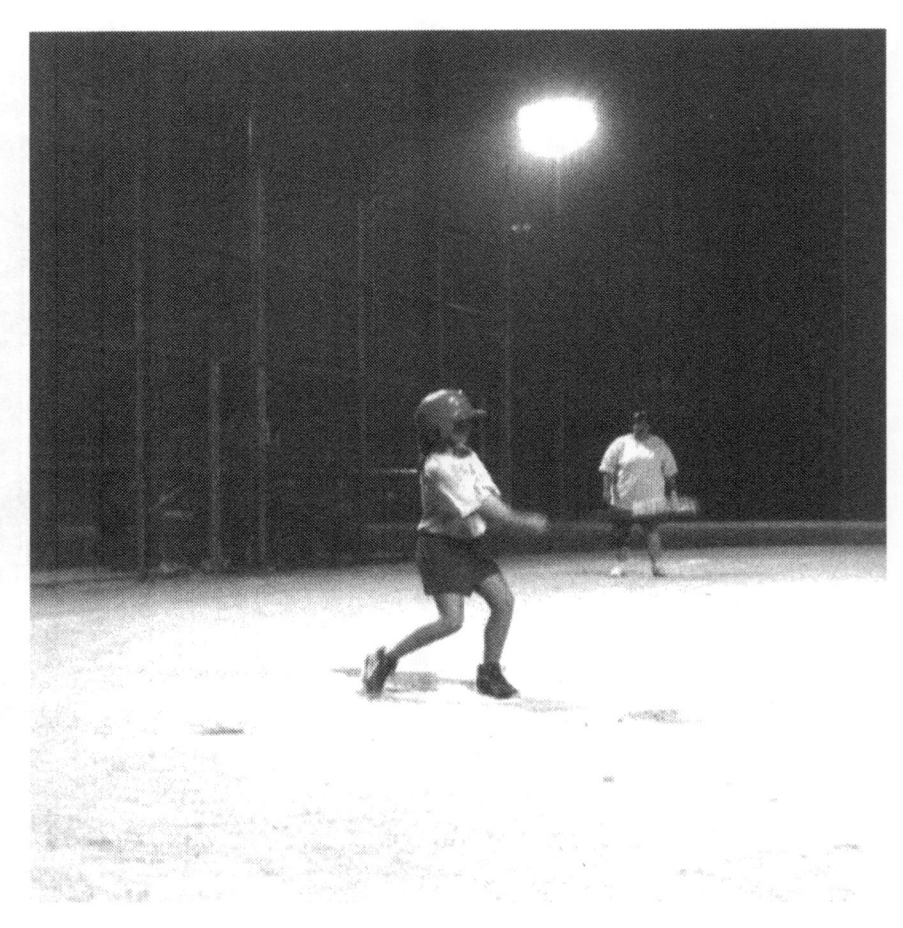

Night Softball; Moberly, Missouri, 2006

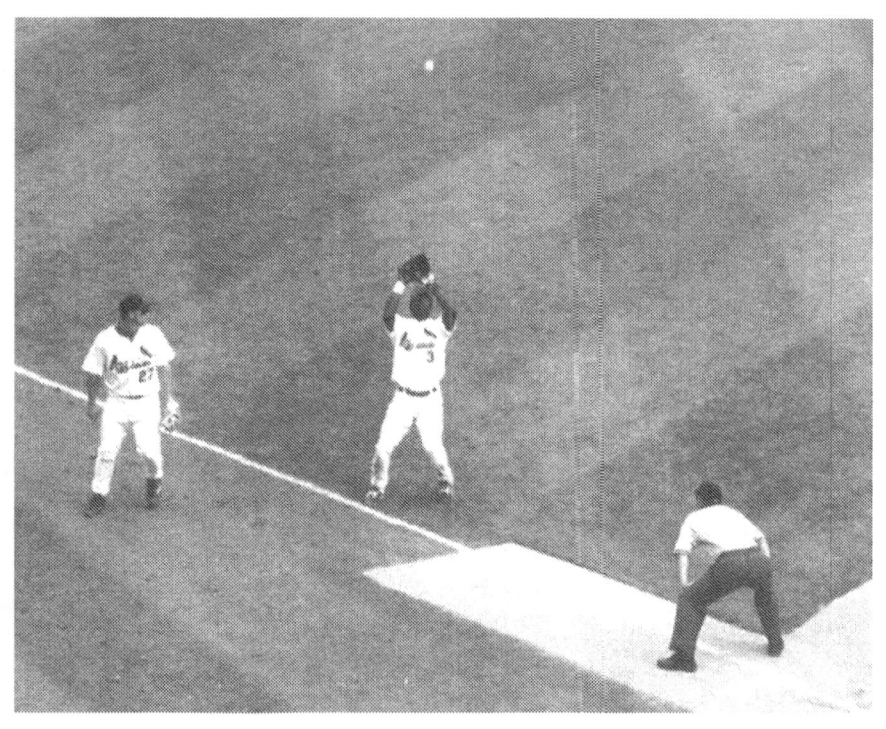

"Fair Or Foul?" St. Louis, Missouri, 2004

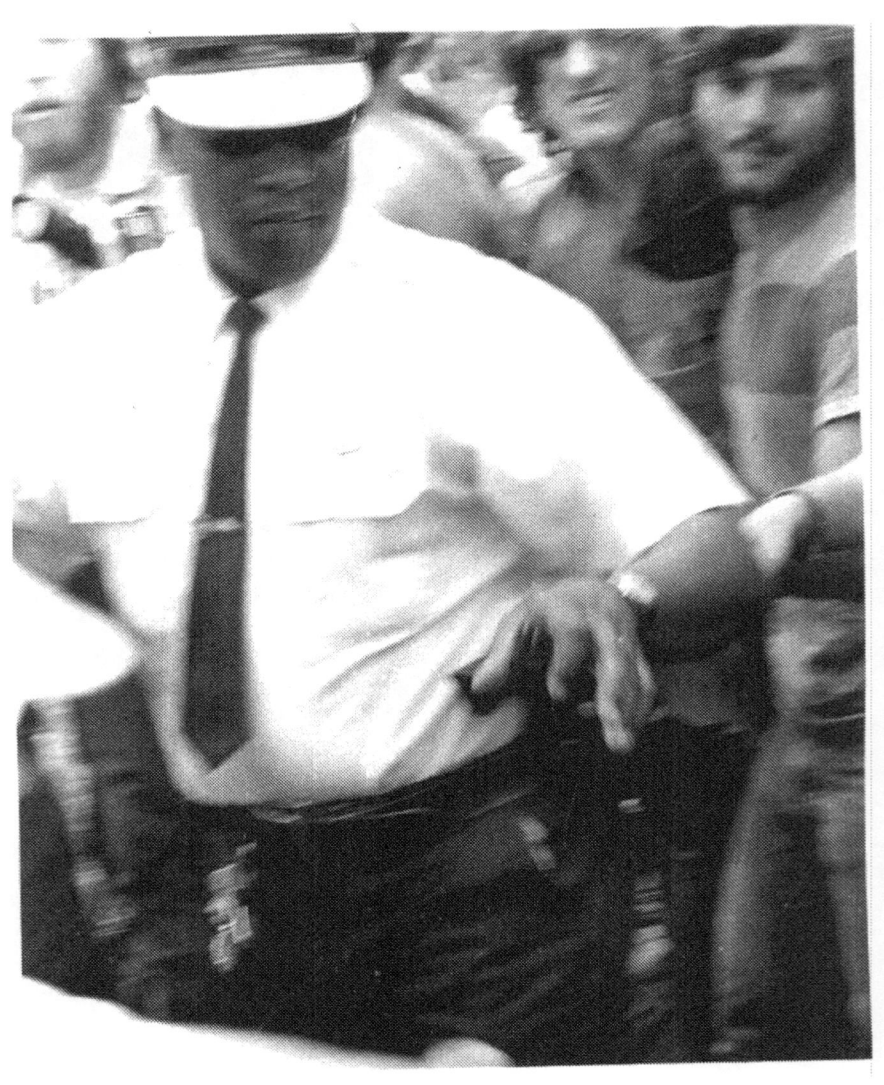

Pot Bust; Cincinnati, Ohio, 1970

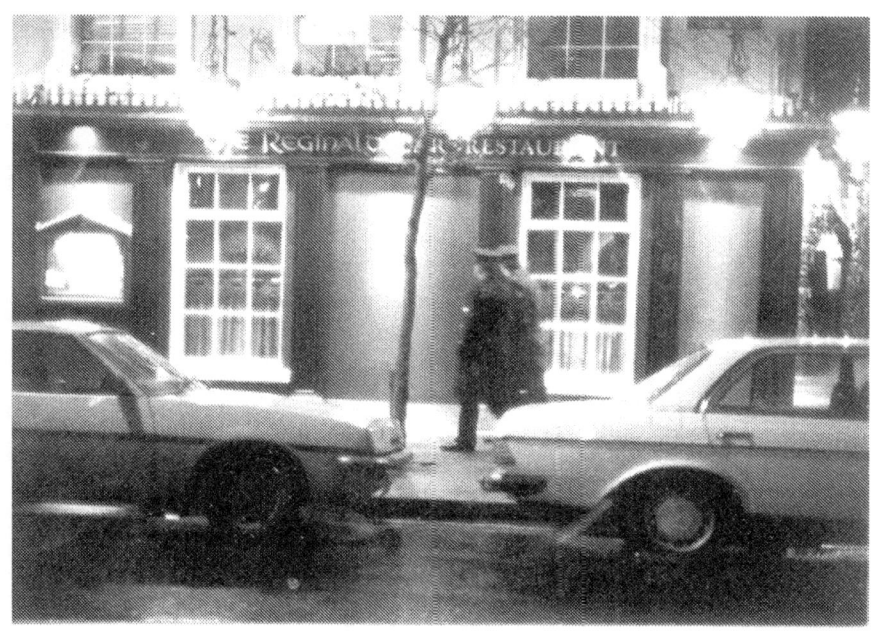

Night Beat in Old Waterford; Ireland, 1989

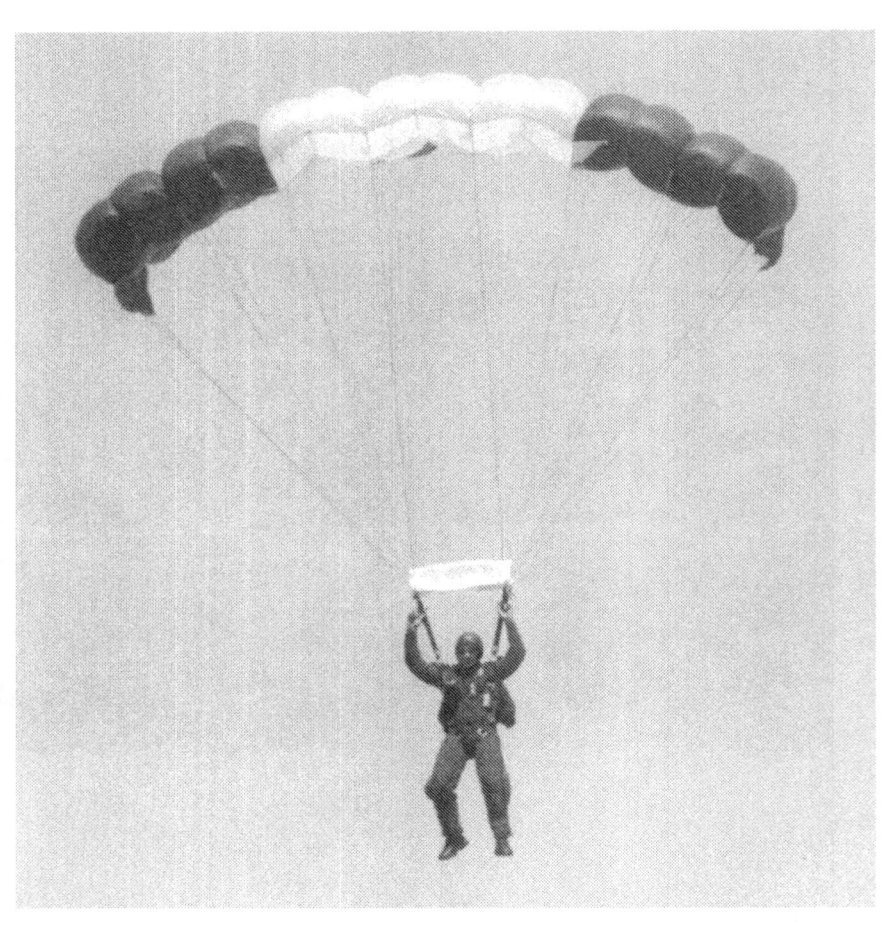

Parachutist; Columbia, Missouri, 2005

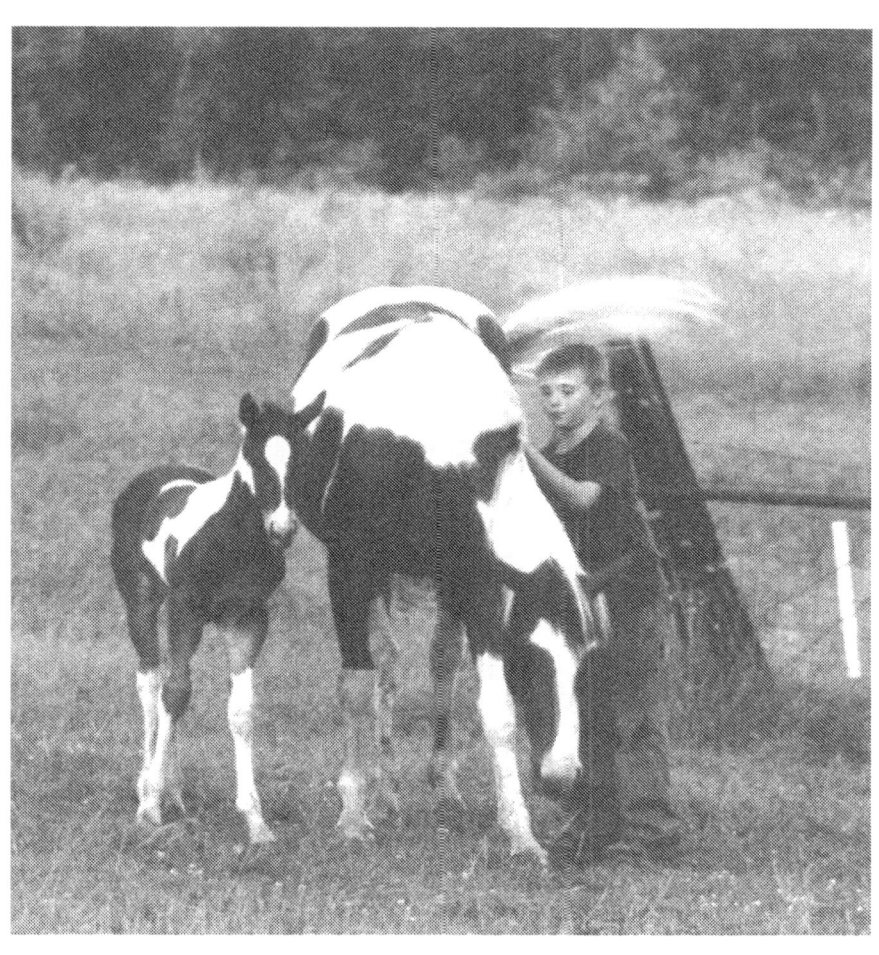

Boy With Mare and Foal, Rural Missouri, 2005

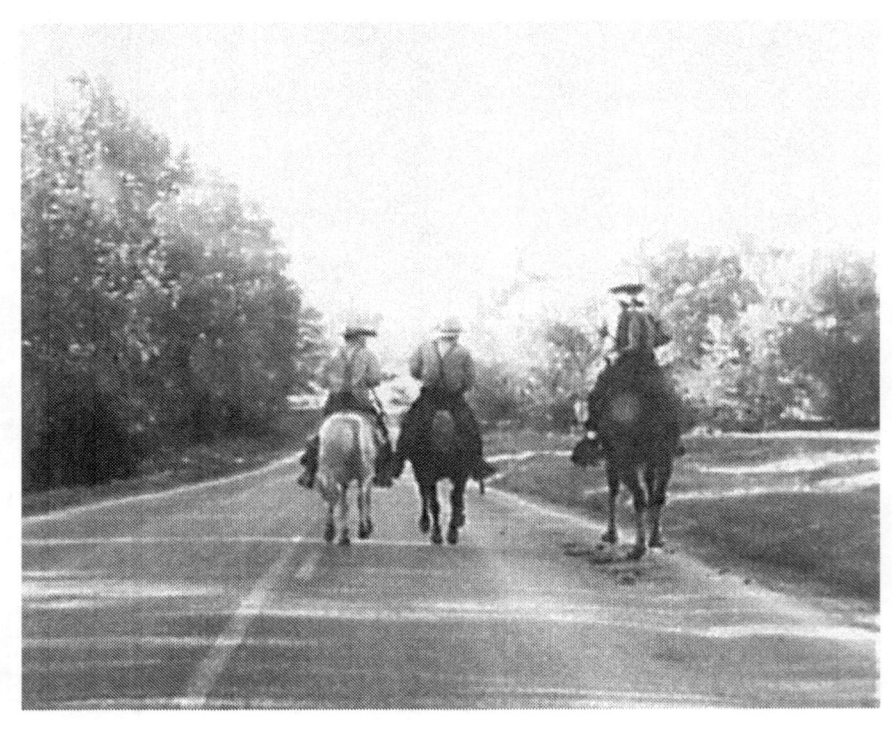

Riding To School; Clark, Missouri, 2004

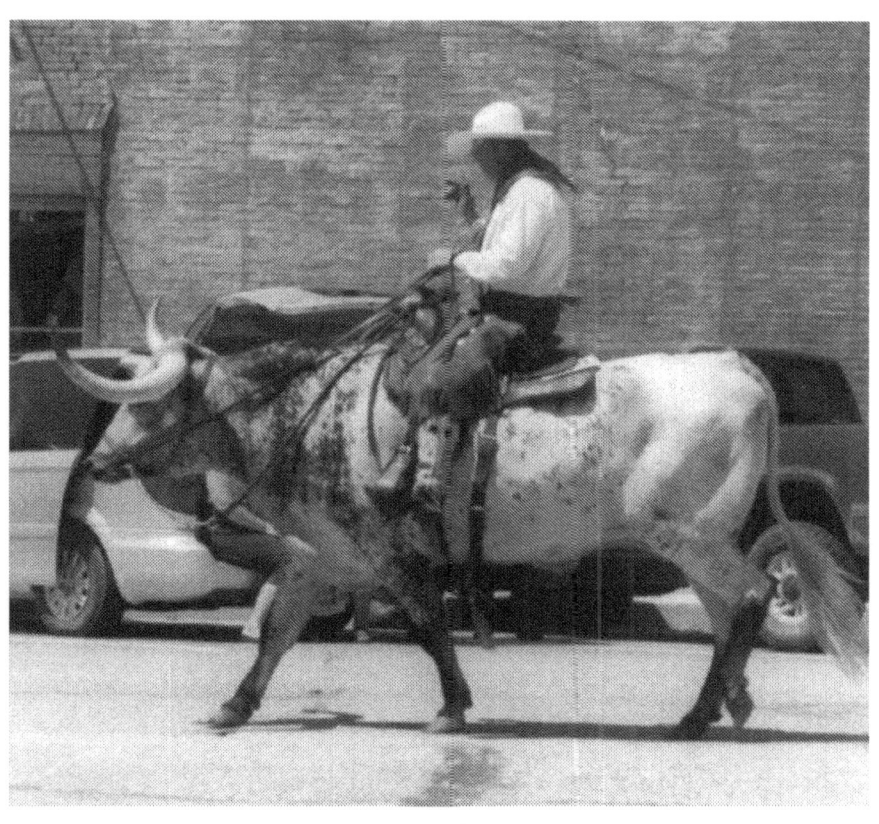

"Yep, A REAL Cowboy," Shelbina, Missouri, 2007

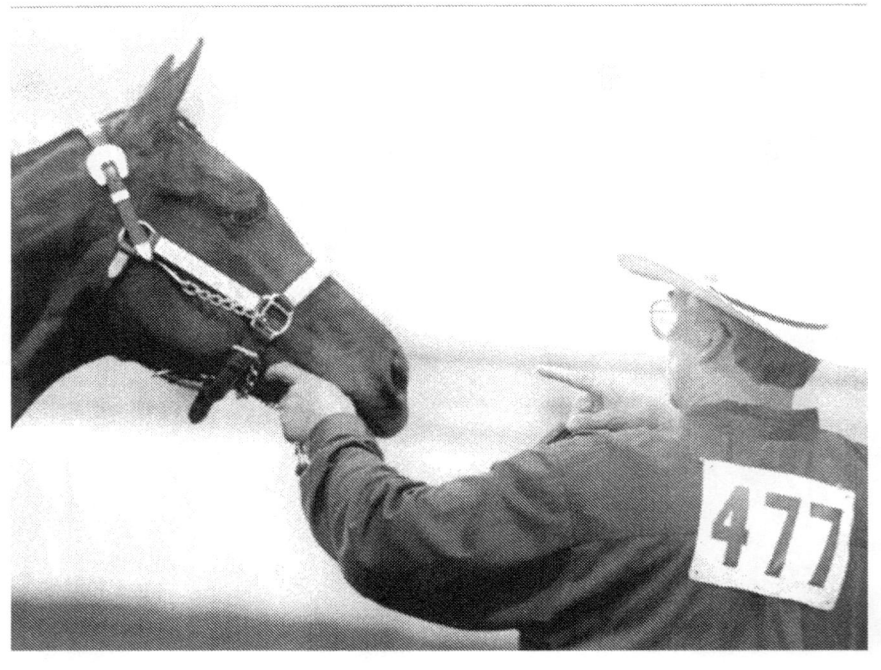

"Behave," Columbia, Missouri, 1992

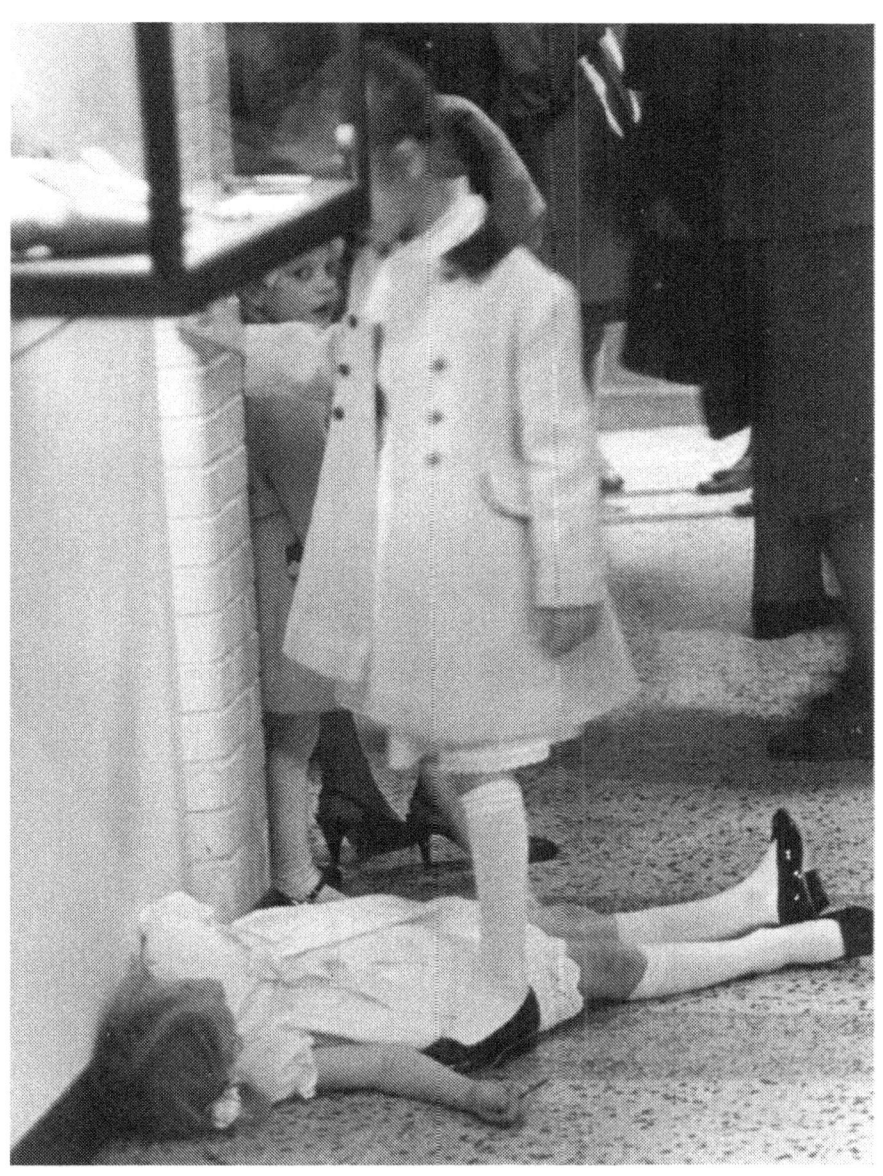

"Acting Up," Williamsburg, Virginia, 1983

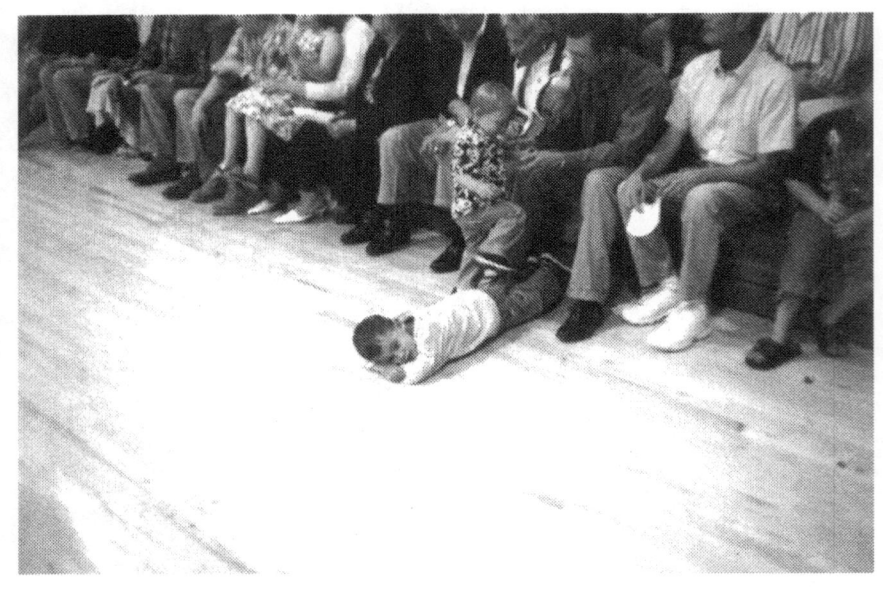

HS Graduation, Madison, Missouri, 2005

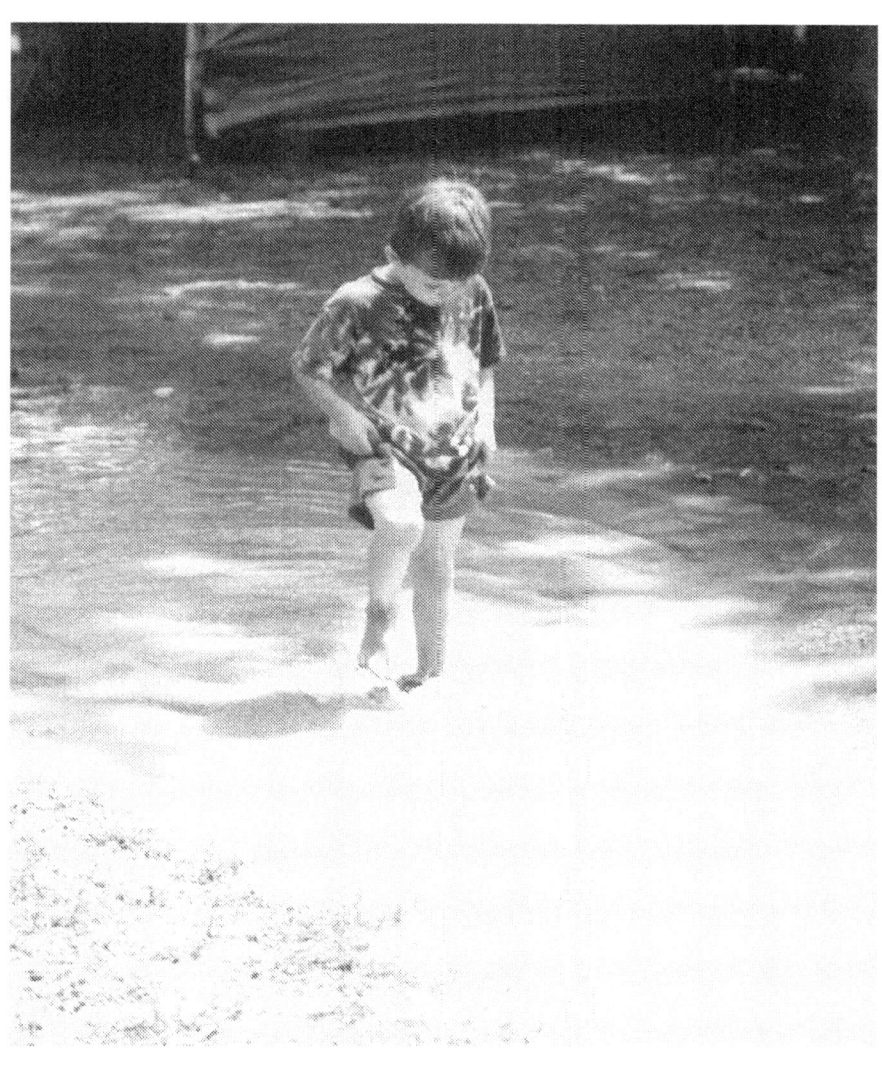

Puddle; Osage Beach, Missouri, 2001

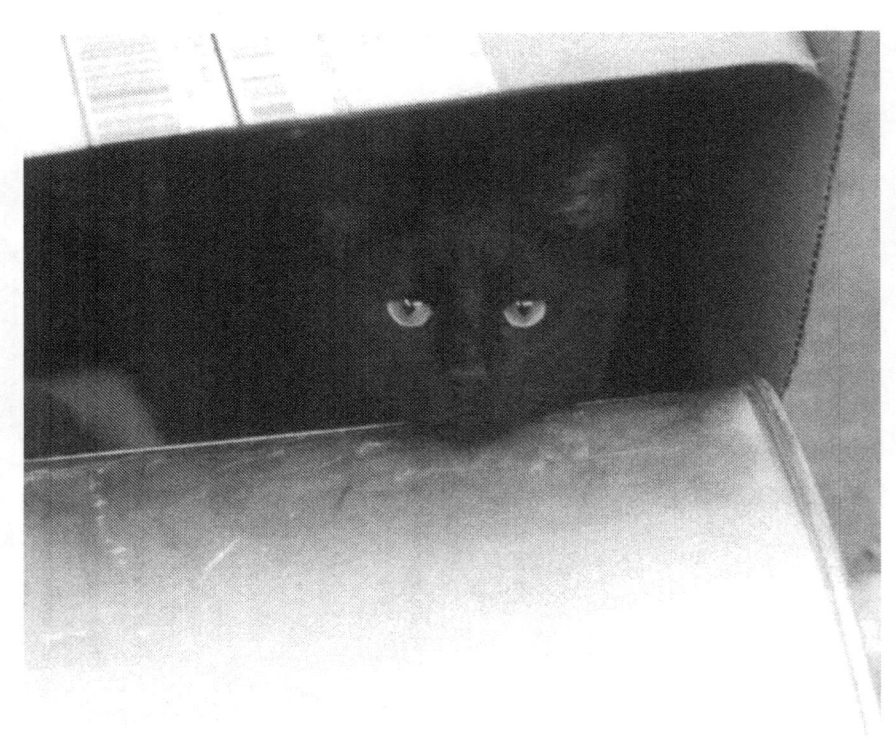

Cat With New Muffler; Columbia, Missouri 2005

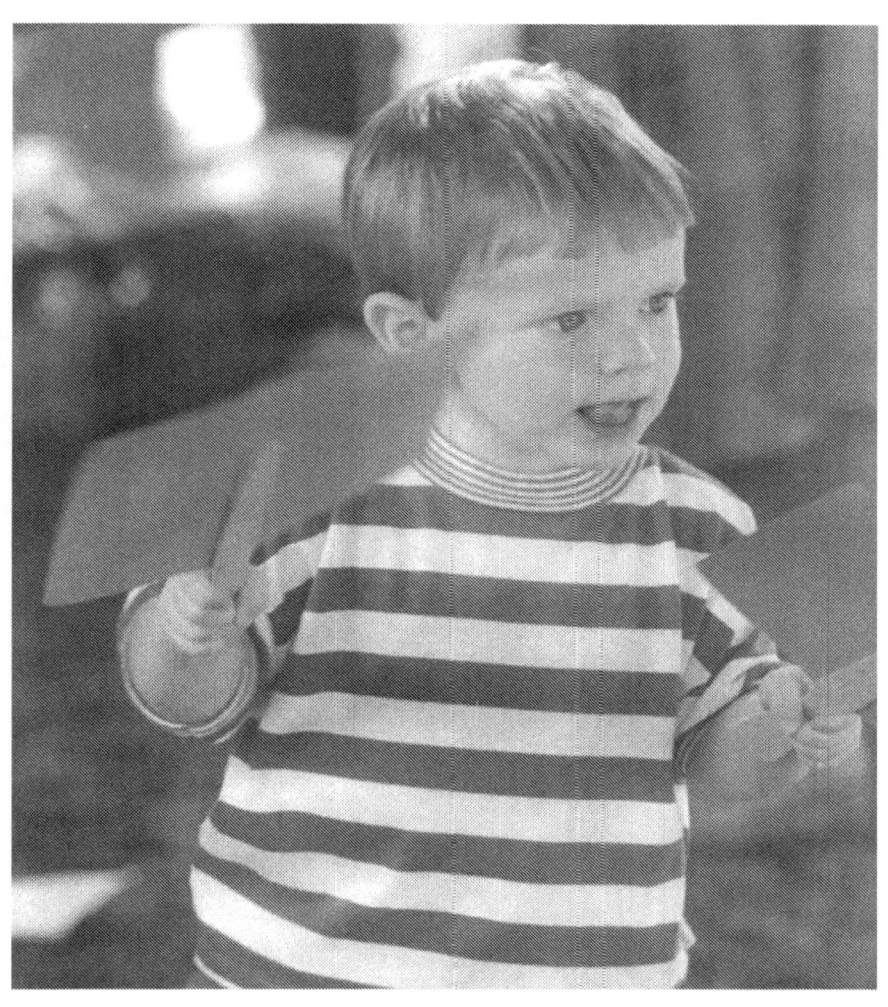

Political Rally; Paris, Missouri, 1994

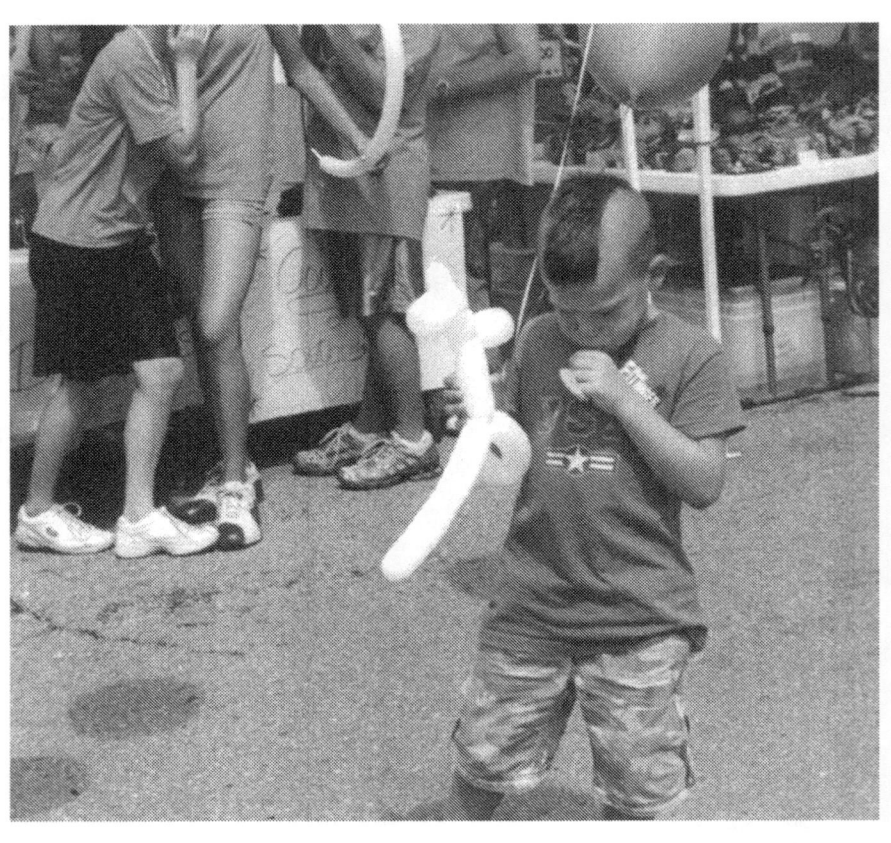

Street Scene; Jefferson City, Missouri, 2005

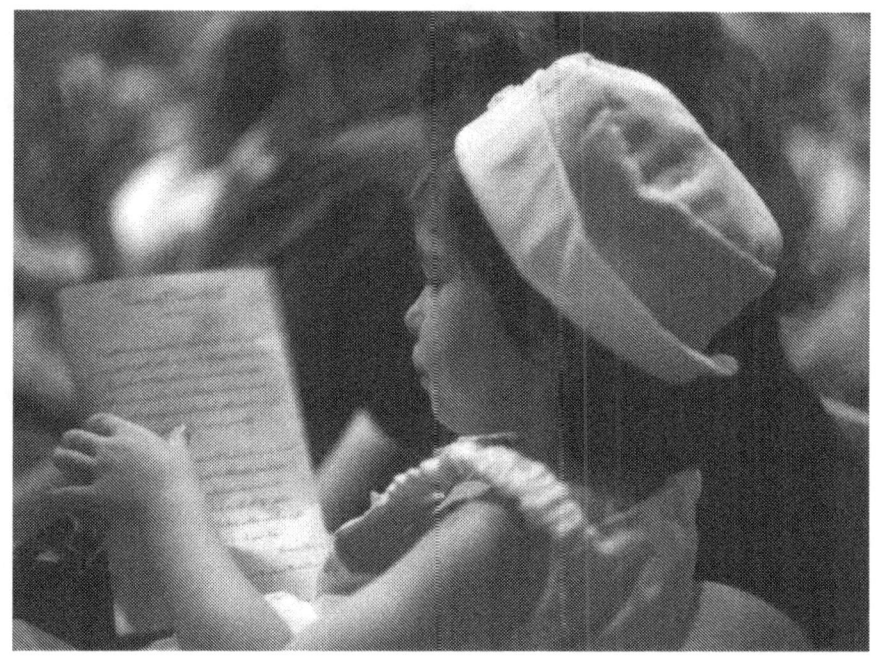

"The Reader," Moberly, Missouri, 2005

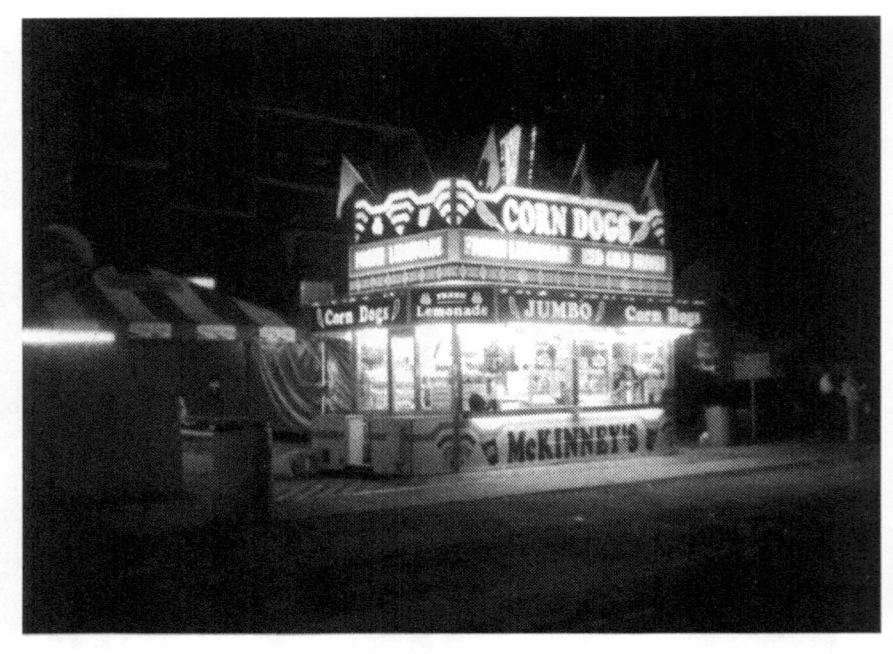

"Corn Dogs," Boone County Fair, Columbia, Missouri, 2004

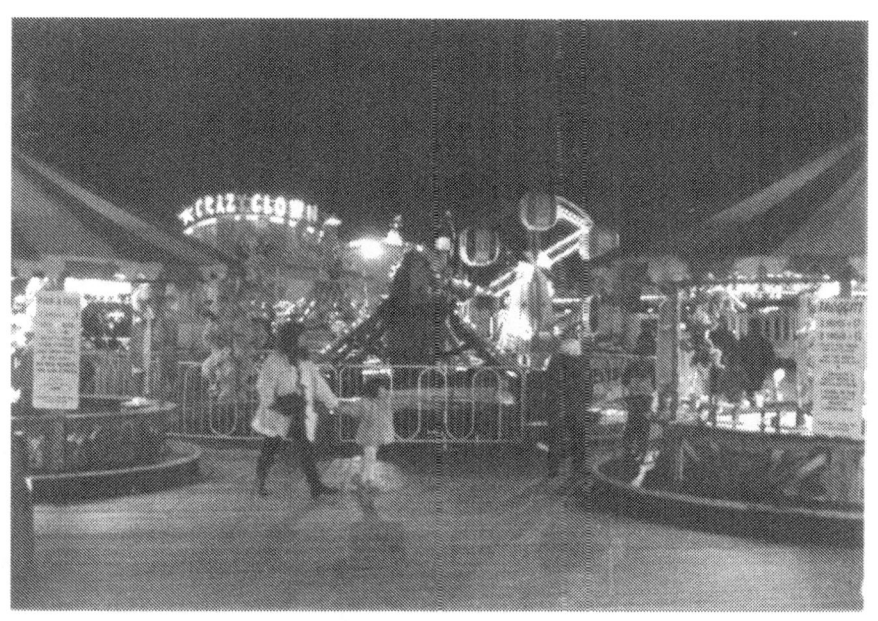

"A Night on Brighton Pier," Brighton, UK, 2002

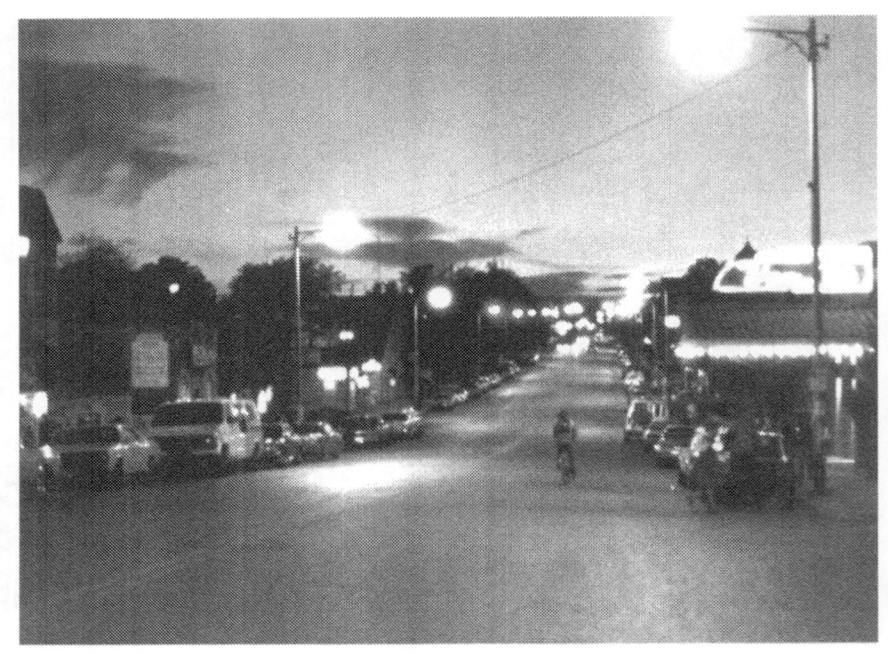

Biking At Night; Bloomington, Indiana, 1984

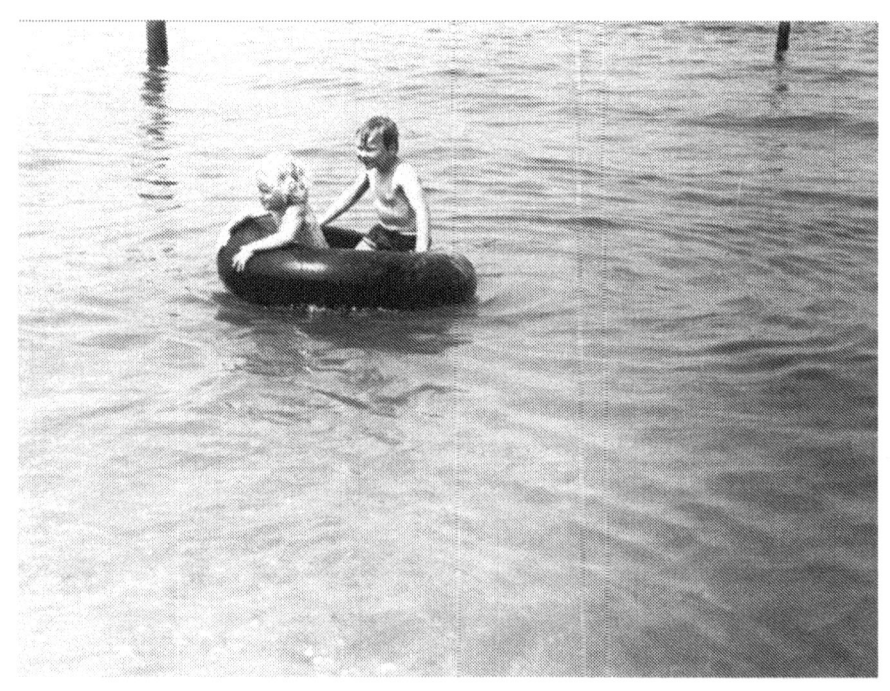

The Innertube, Newport News, Virginia, 1983

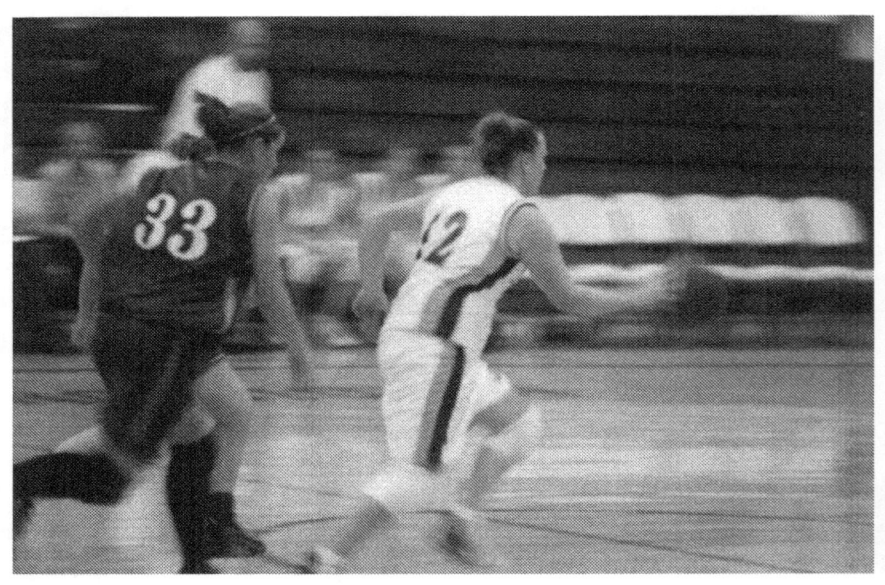

"Downcourt," Madison, Missouri, 2006

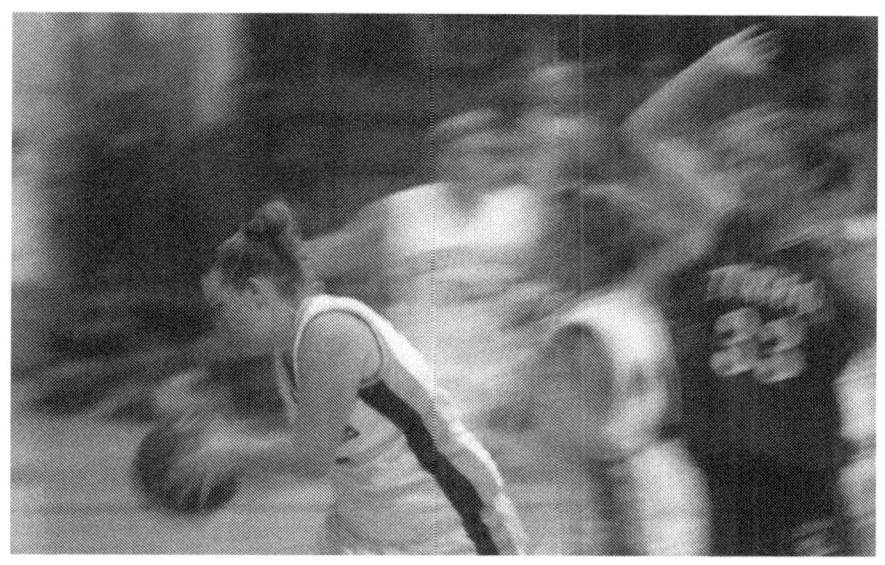

"The Quiet Moment At The Center Of The Action," Madison, Missouri, 2006

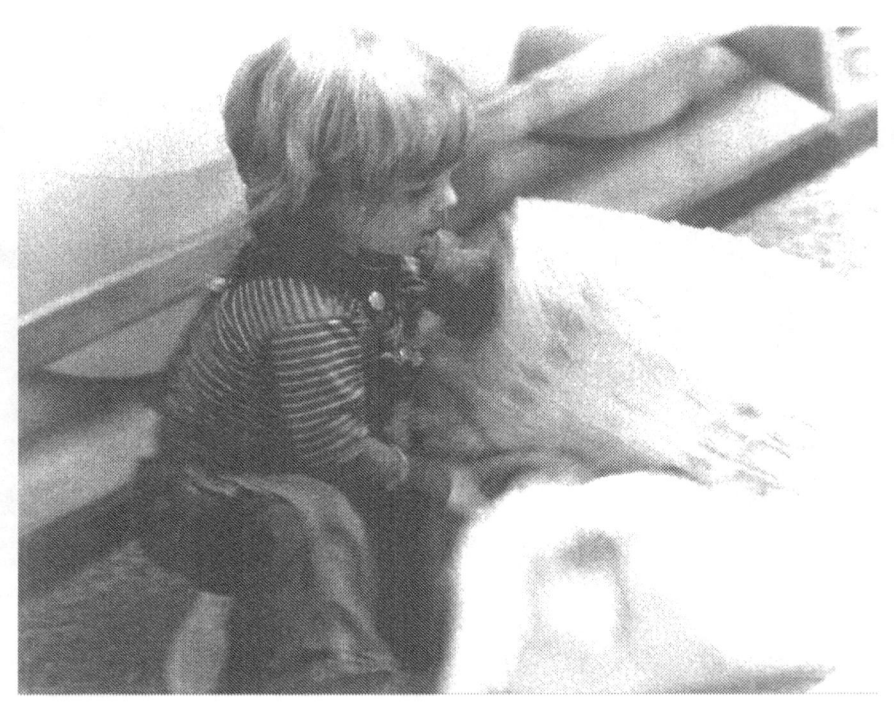

Favorite Blanket, Williamsburg, Virginia, 1984

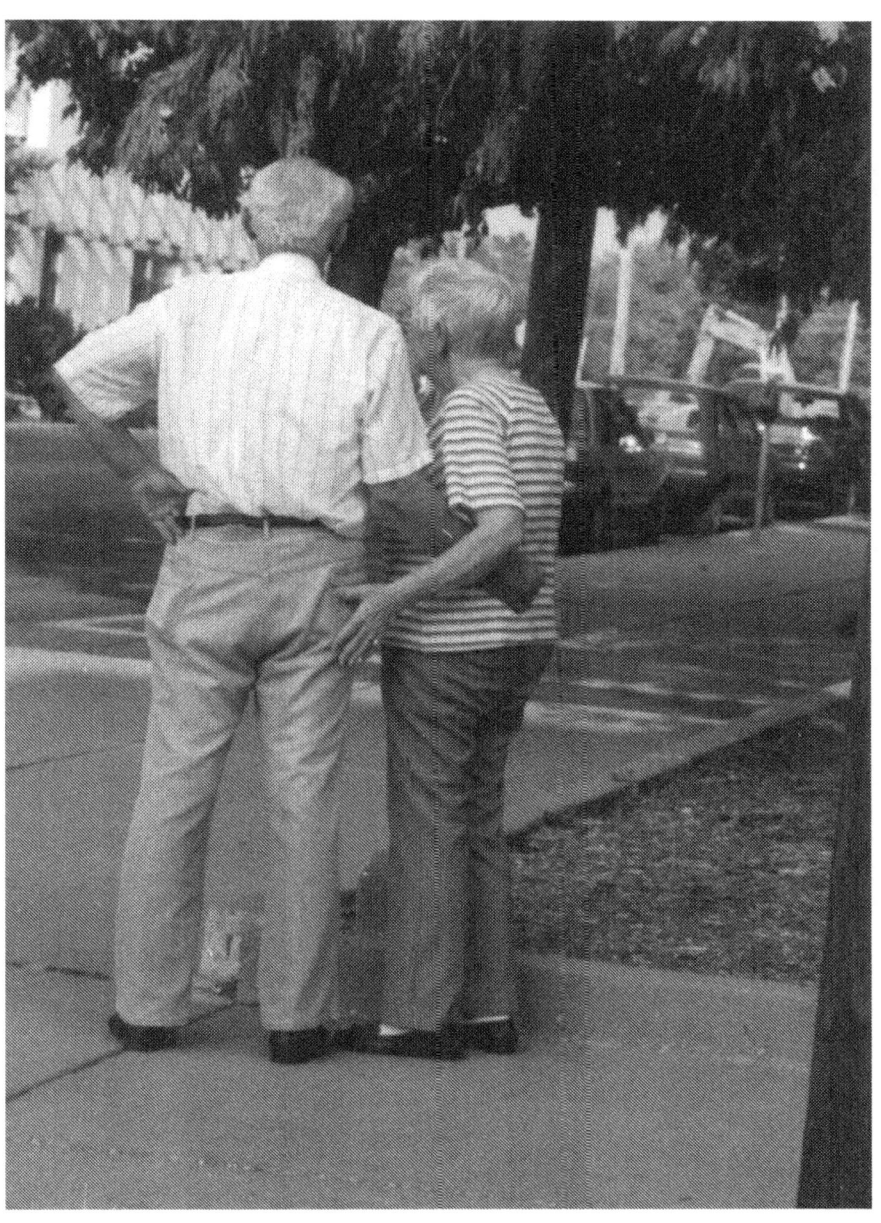

"You're Never Too Old," Columbia, Missouri, 1999

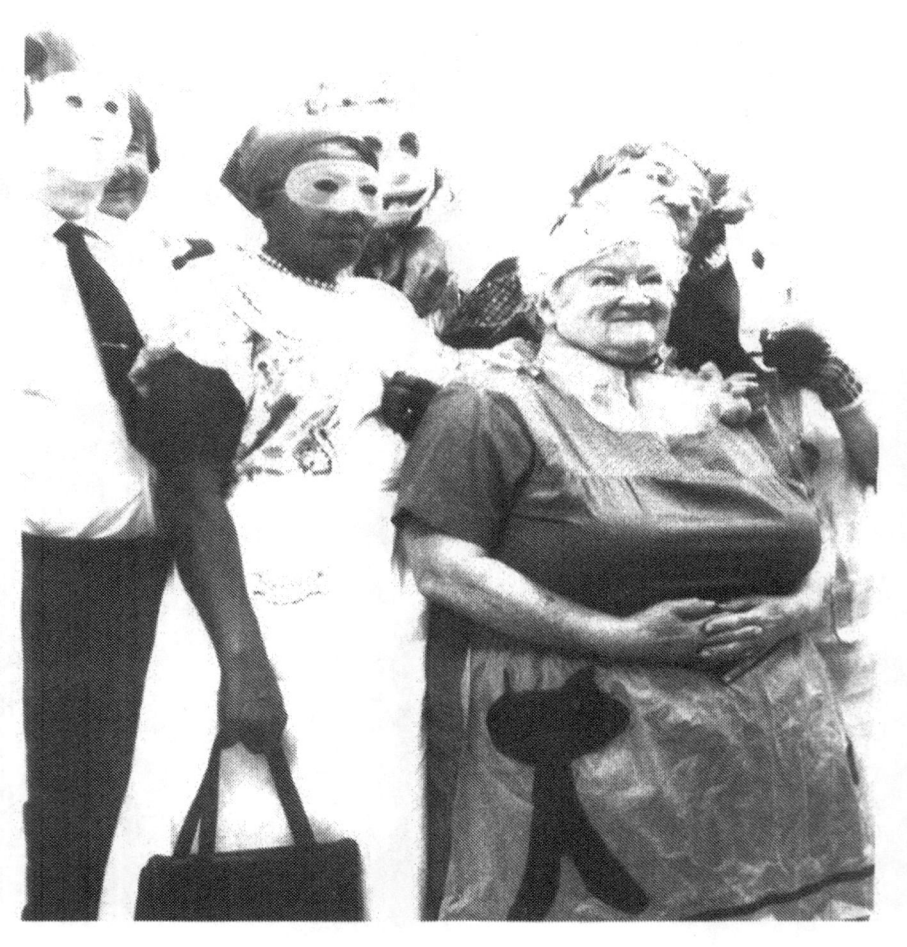

"You're Never Too Old..." Cincinnati, Ohio, 1973

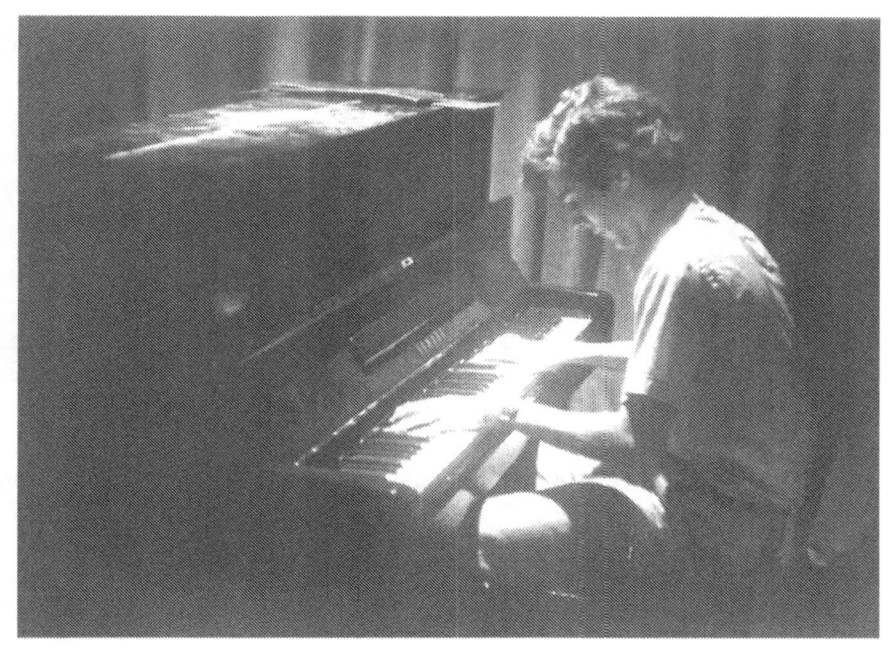

Practicing; Williamsburg, Virginia, 1984

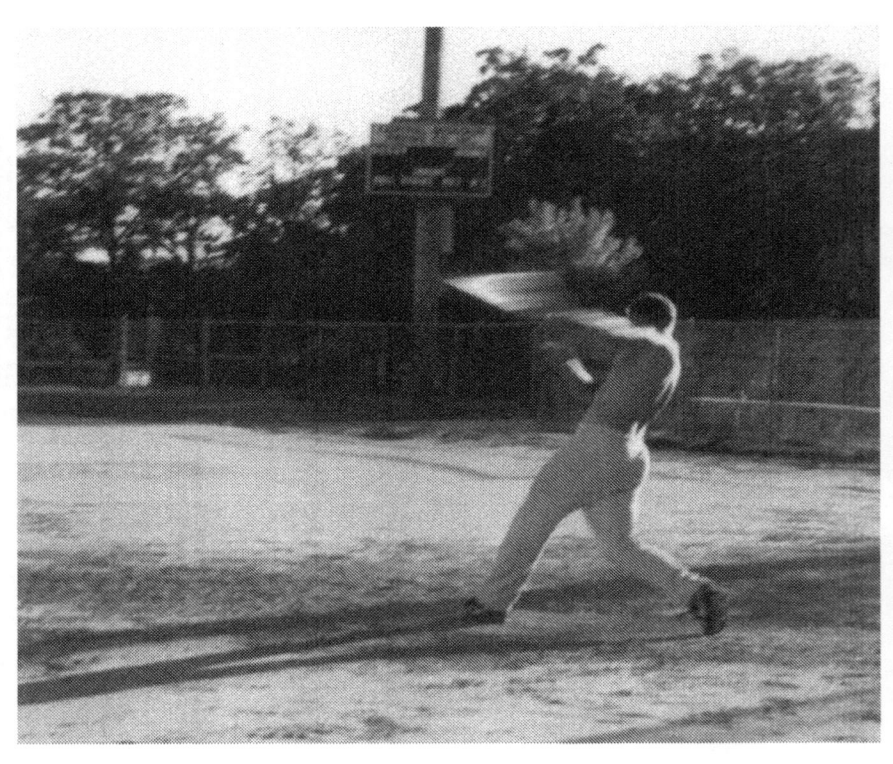

"A Good Full Swing," Moberly, Missouri, 2006

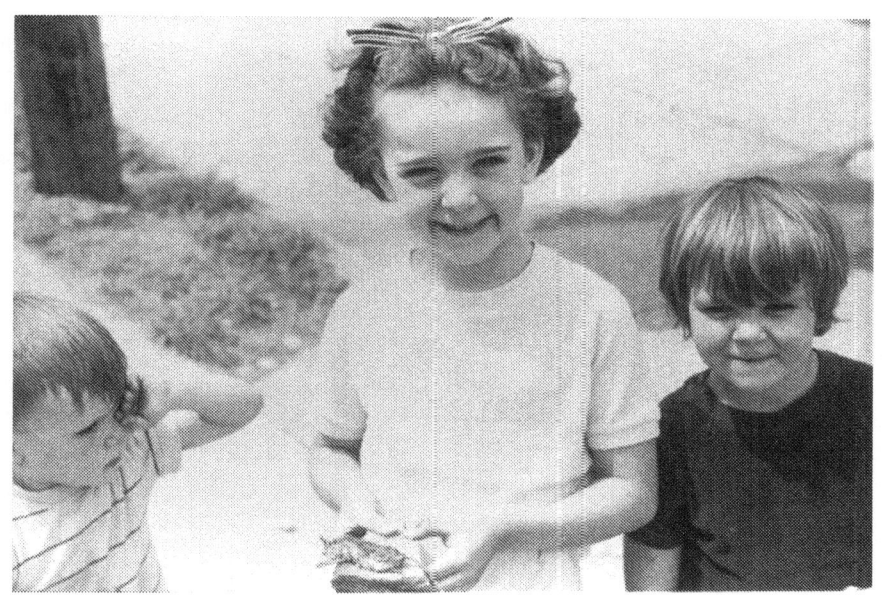

"Look What WE Have!" Fort Thomas, Kentucky, 1972 *(A dead mouse)*

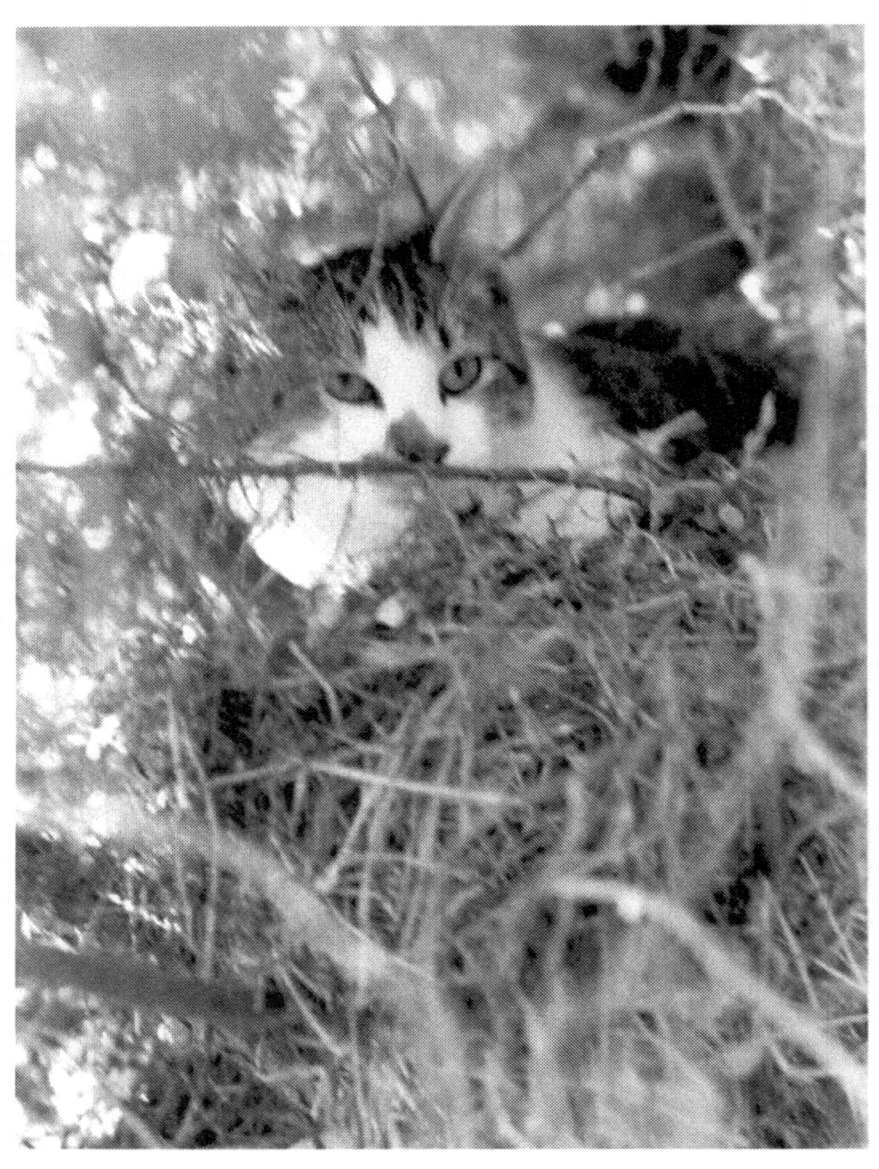

Contented Cat; Middle Grove, Missouri, 1988

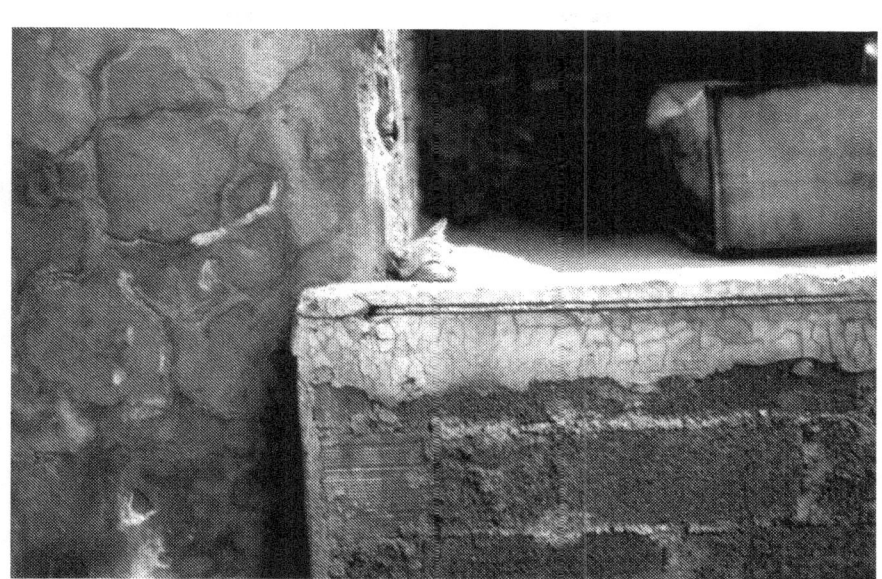

Cat Sleeping In The Sun; Limassol, Cyprus,1987

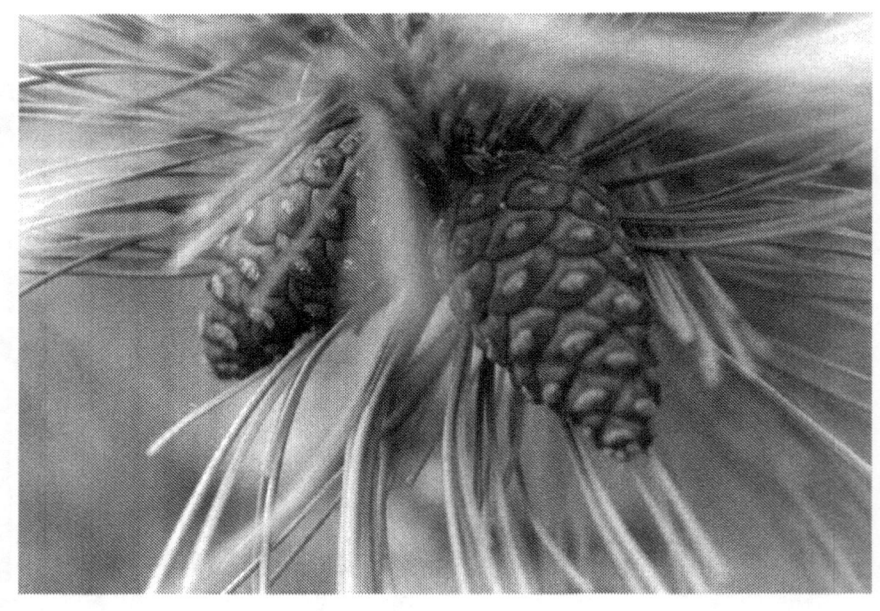

Pinecones; Rural Canada, 2006

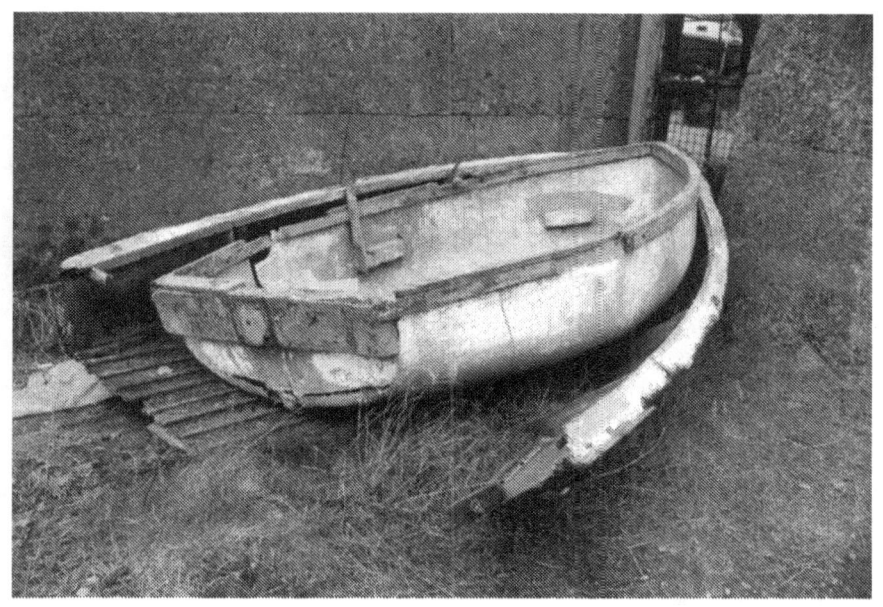

"There Once Was A Boat, Stacked Up On A Boat, For a Very Long Time, Now Neither Will Float..." South Gare, England, 2001

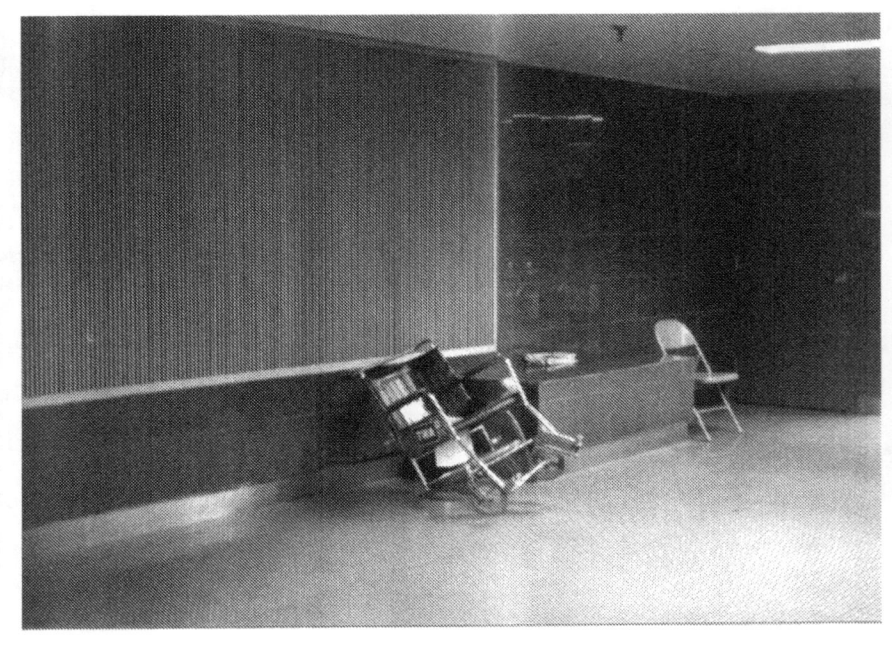

Broken Chair for A Broken Airline; Heathrow, UK, 2001

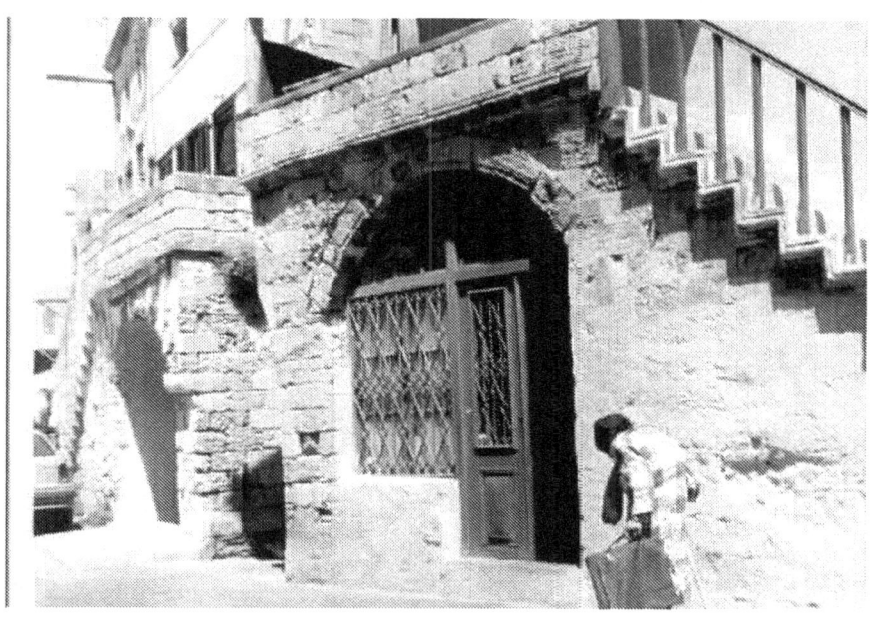

Giagia (granny); Chania, Crete, 1981

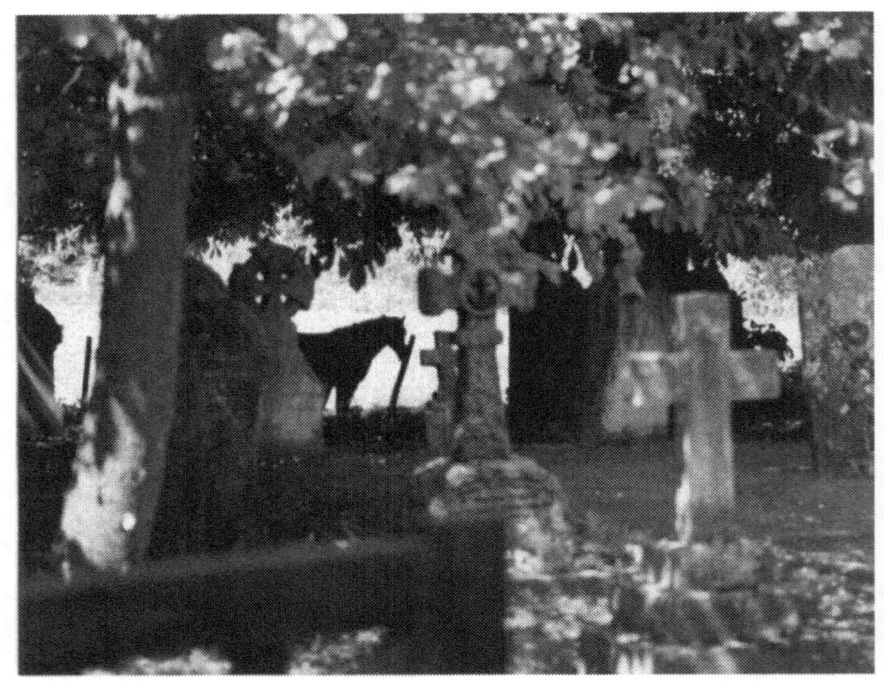

Pony In The Graveyard; Shalebourne, Wiltshire, England, 1984

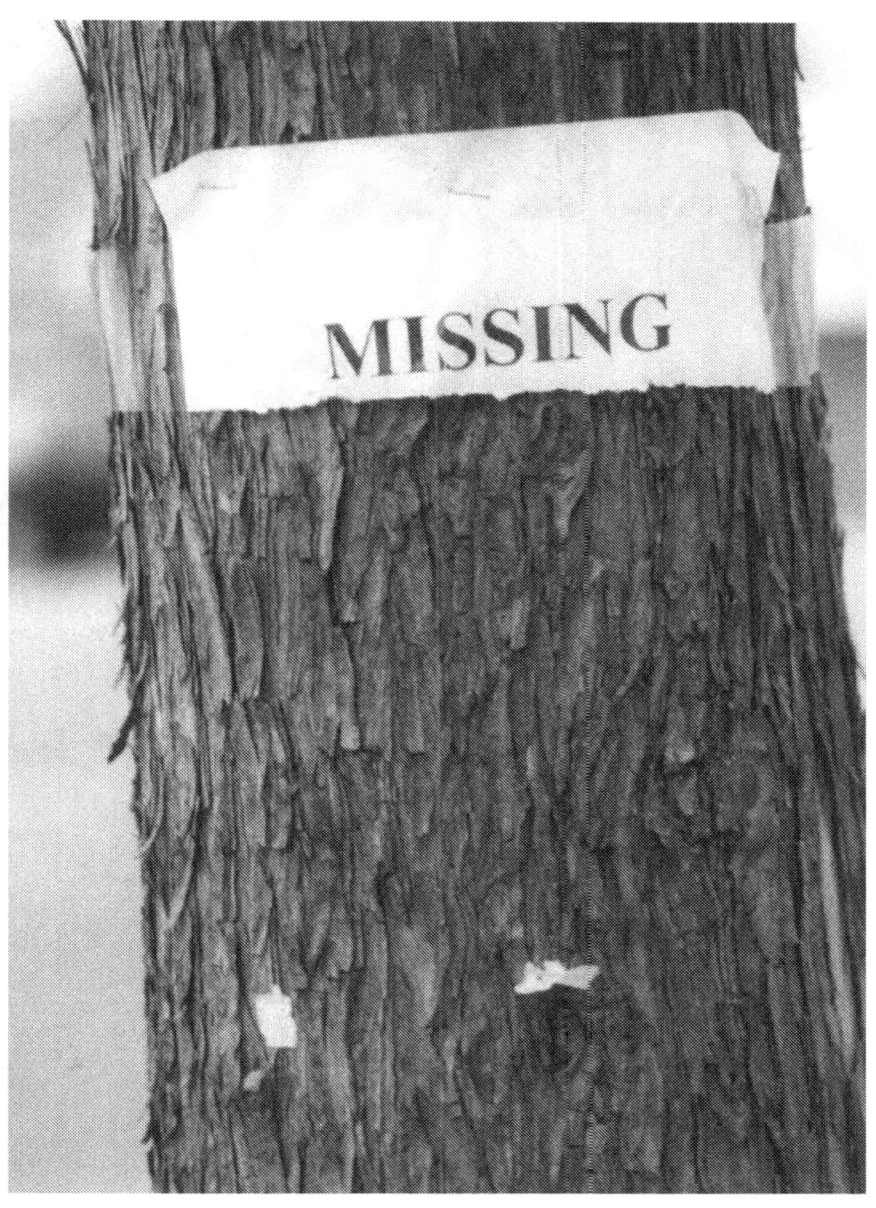

"Something's Missing," Columbia, Missouri, 2007

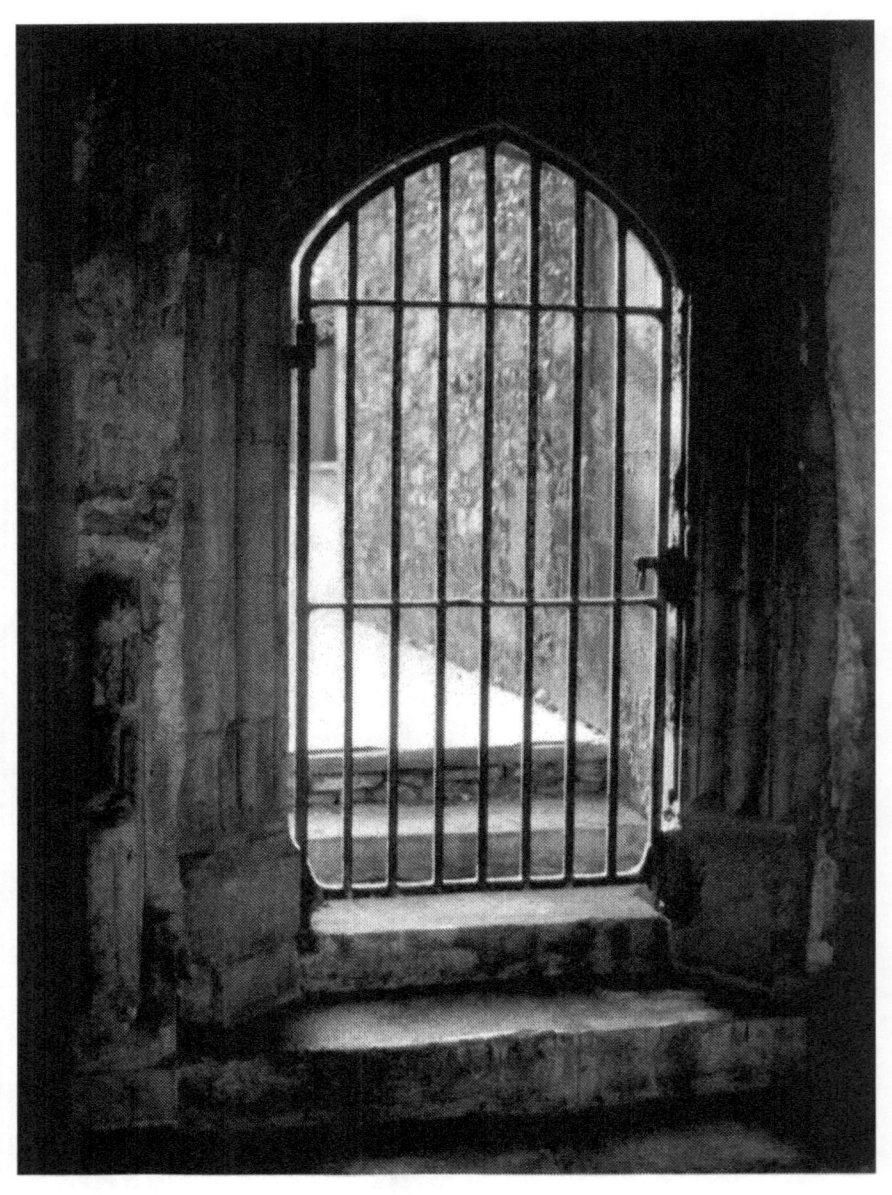

Barred Door; Canterbury, UK, 2000

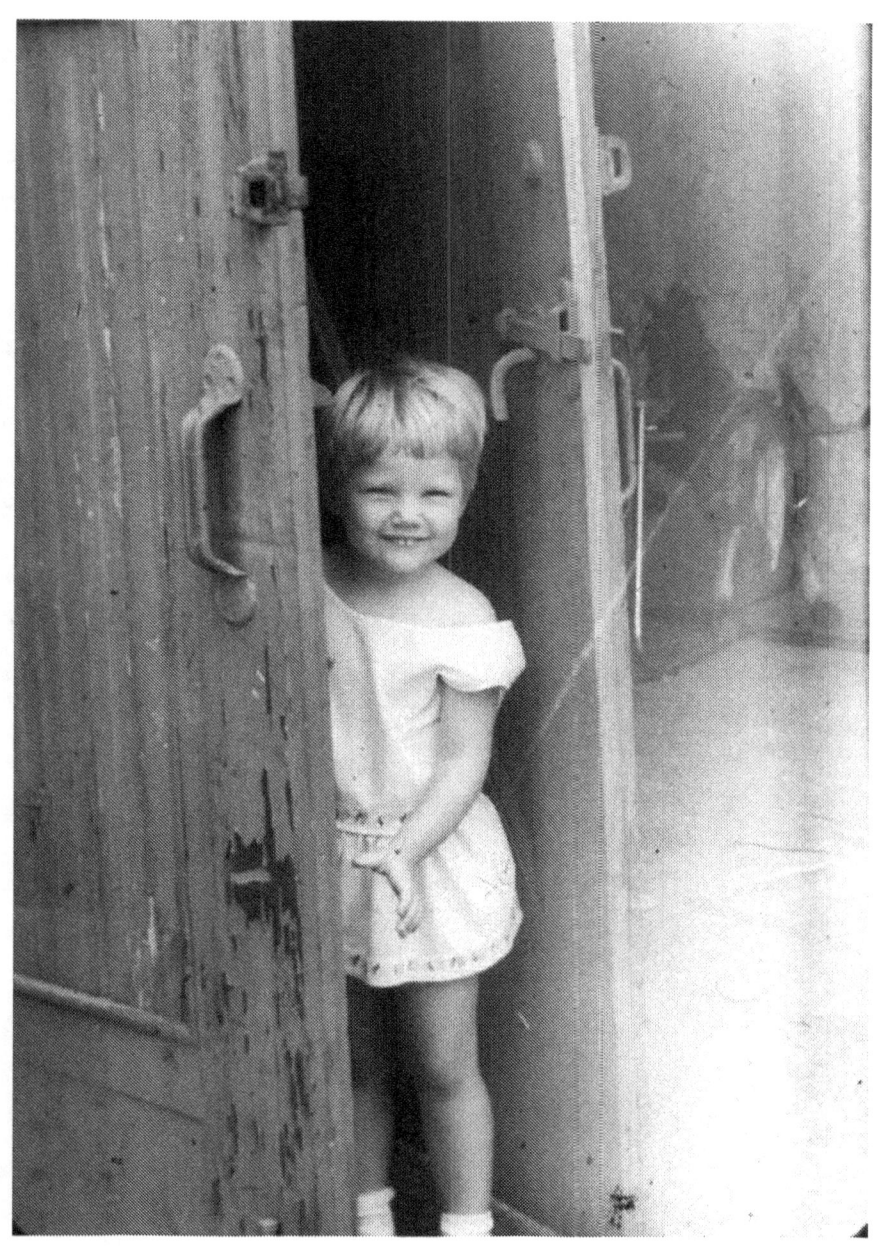

"Come in," Cincinnati, Ohio, 1973

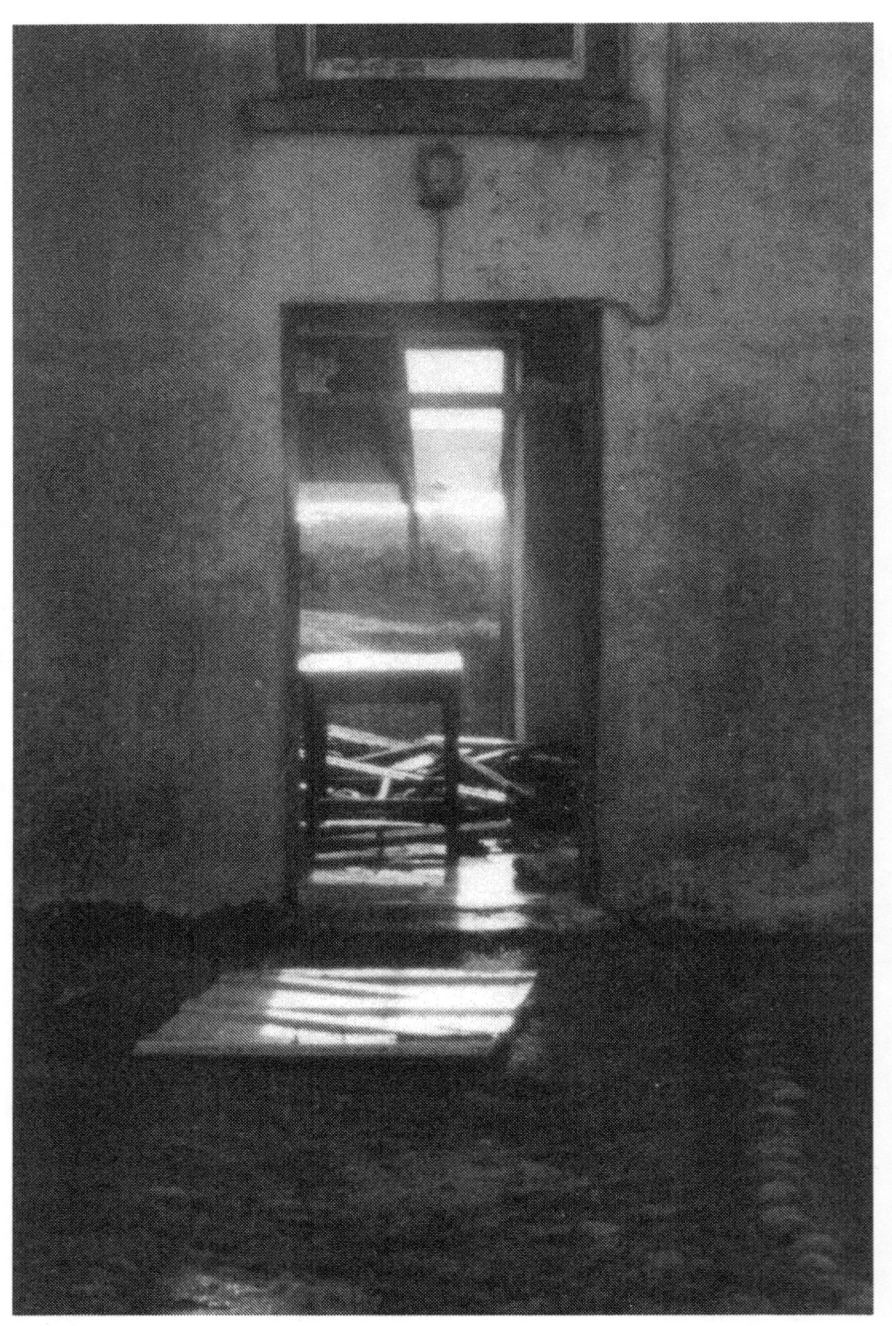

"Sunlight through Open Door," Rural Ireland, 1989

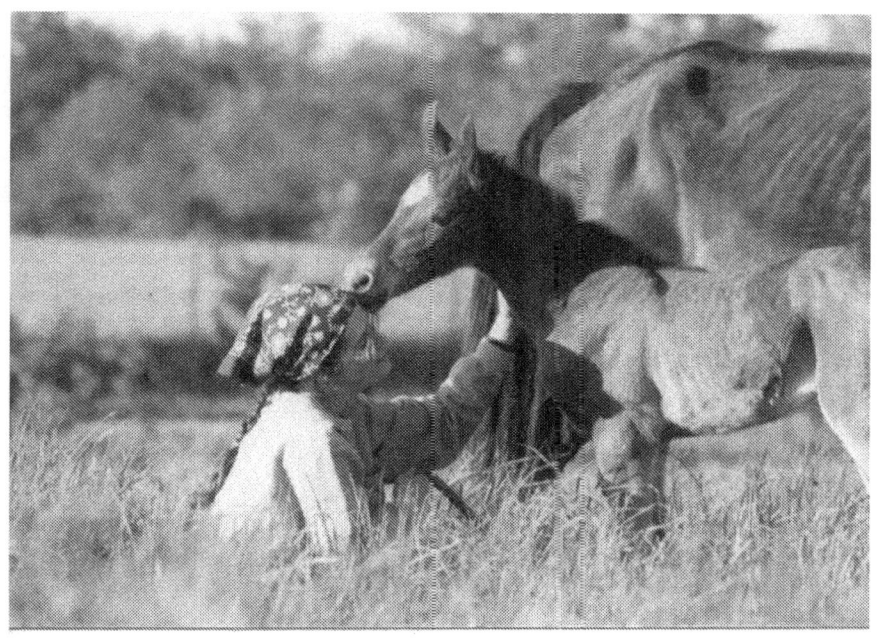

New Foal; Middle Grove, Missouri, 1990

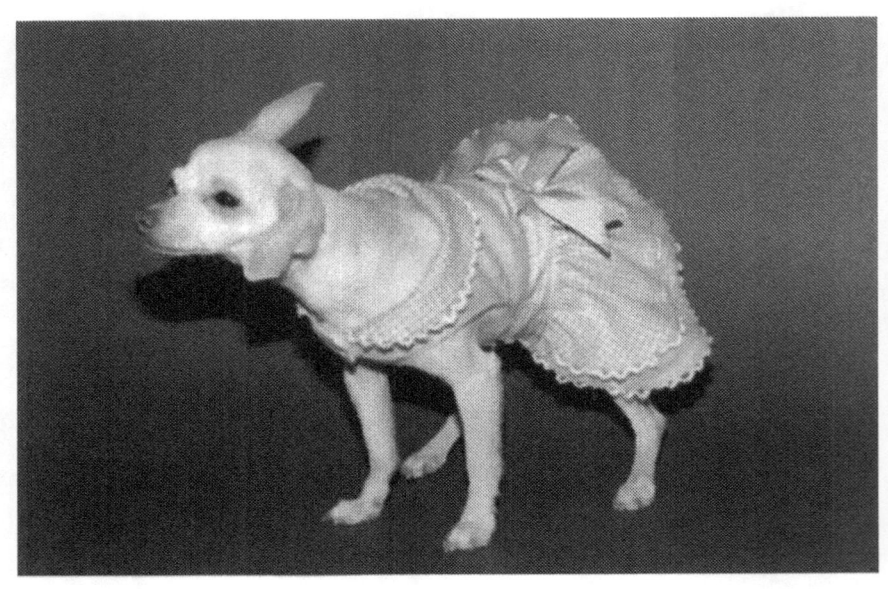

Dog in A Dress; Moberly, Missouri, 2007

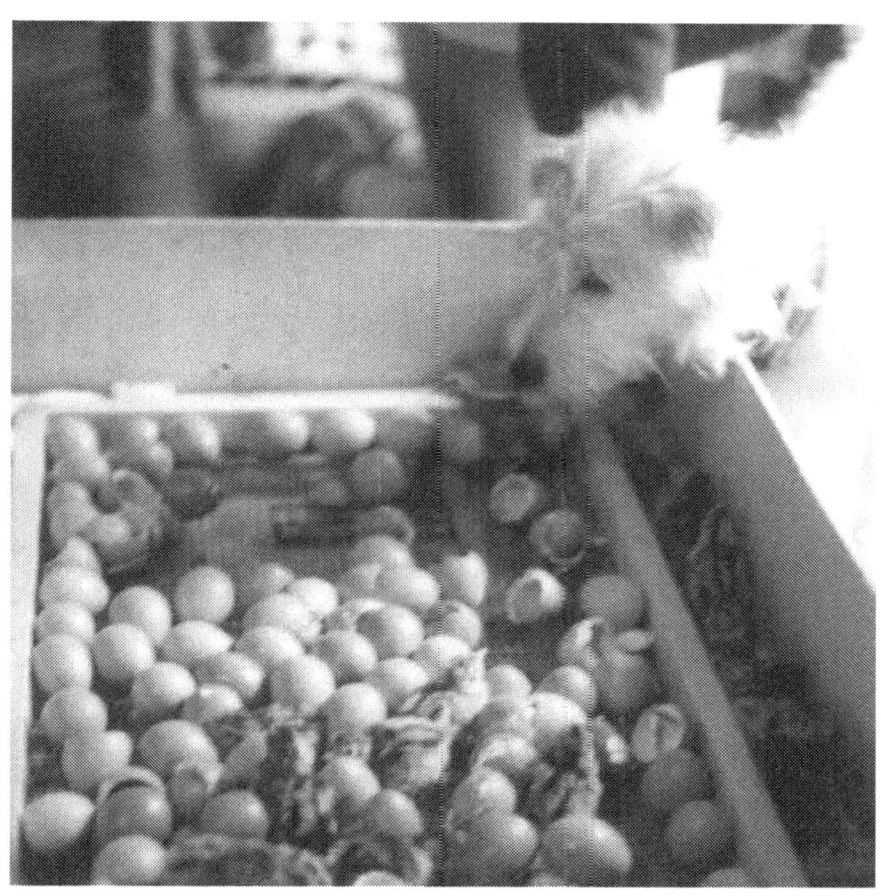

The Miracle of New Life; Great Bedwyn, England, 1984

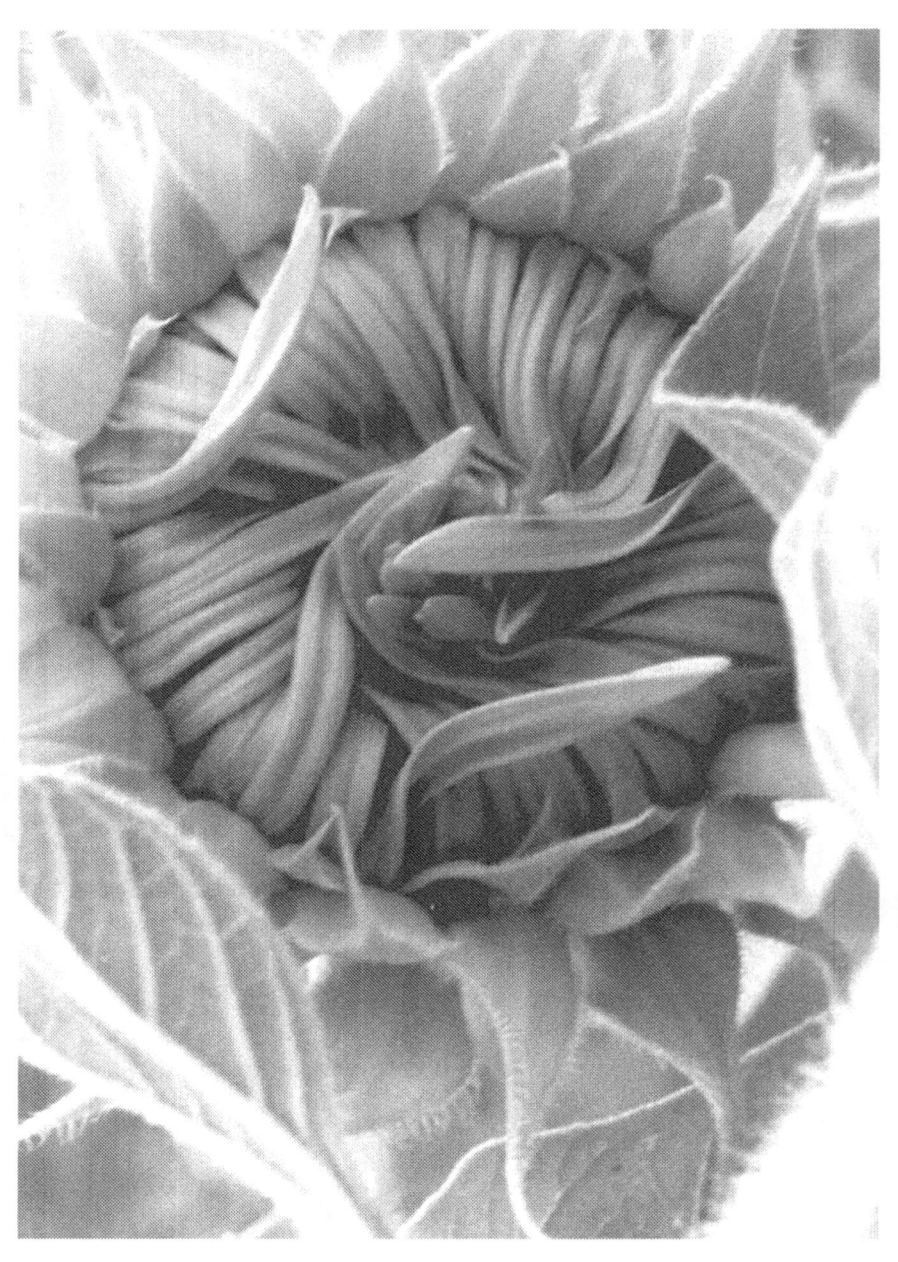

Coy Flower; Moberly, Missouri, 1996

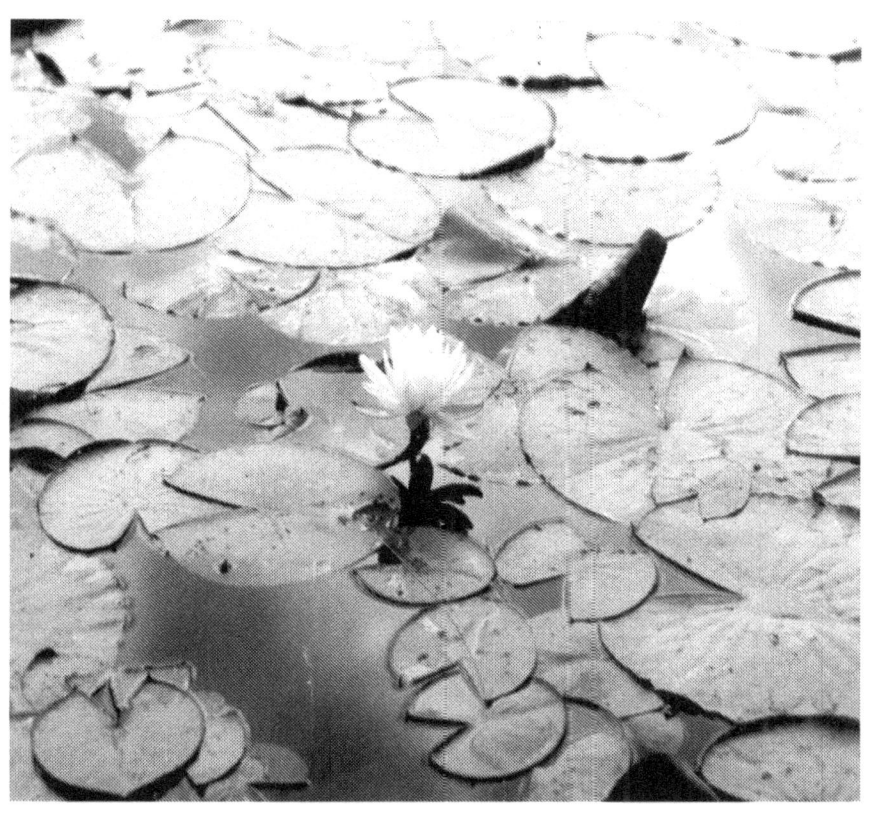

Water Lilies, Moberly, Missouri, 1997

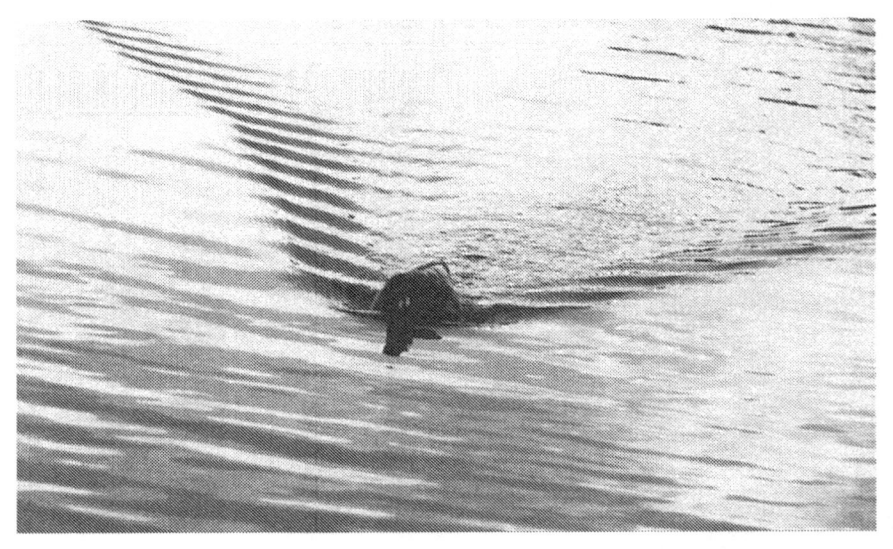

Duck and Wake; Cumbria, UK 2001

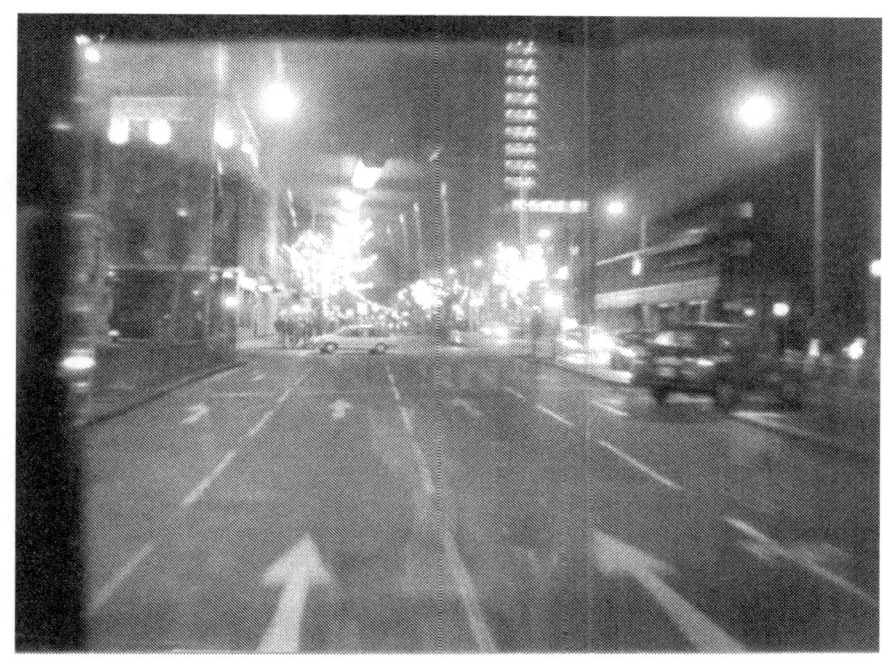

London At Midnight; UK, 2002

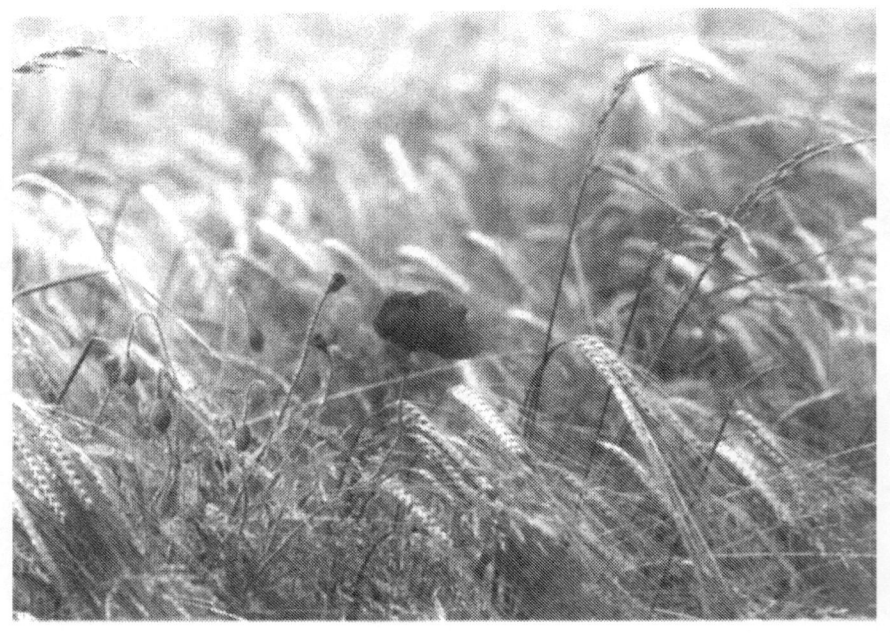

Poppy In The Barley; Lambourn, England, 1988

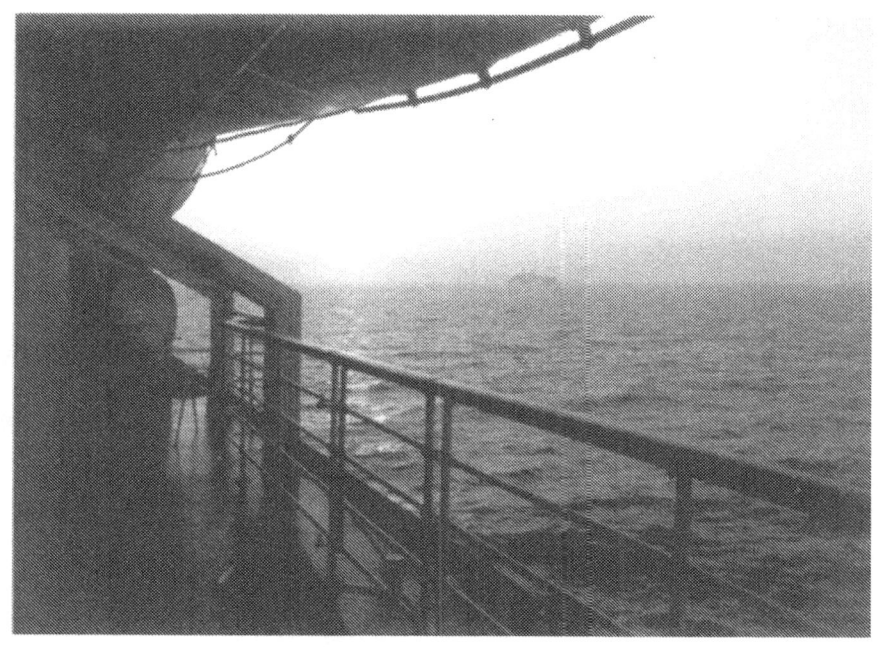

Dawn in the Aegean Sea; off Athens, Greece, 1987

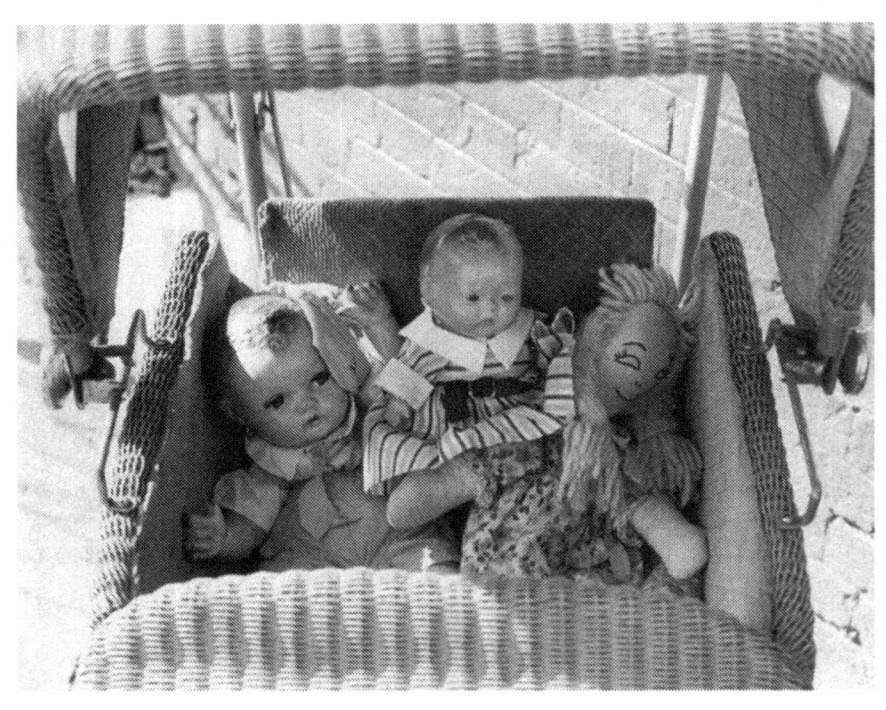

Dollies in a Cart; Williamsburg, Virginia, 1984

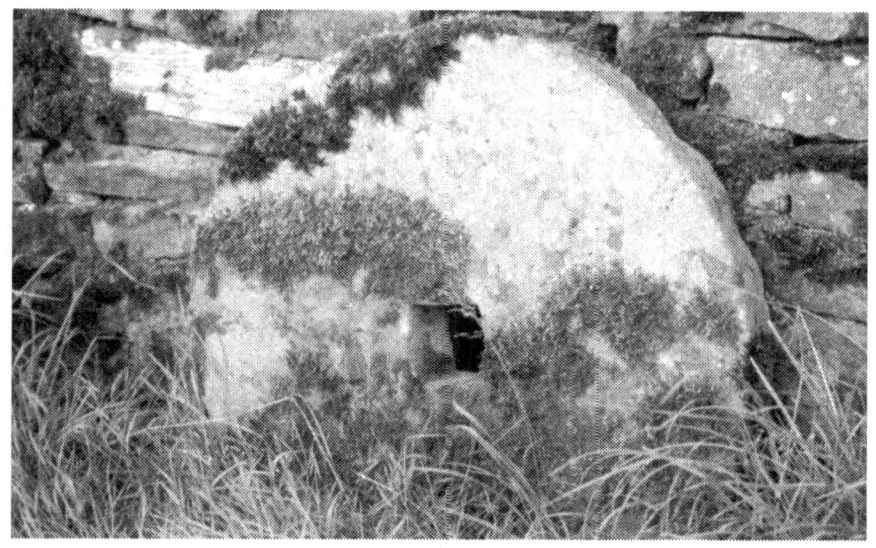

Millstone; Howgill, Hallbankgate, Brampton, Cumbria, UK, 1990
(and this is the original "millstone around your neck" as well)

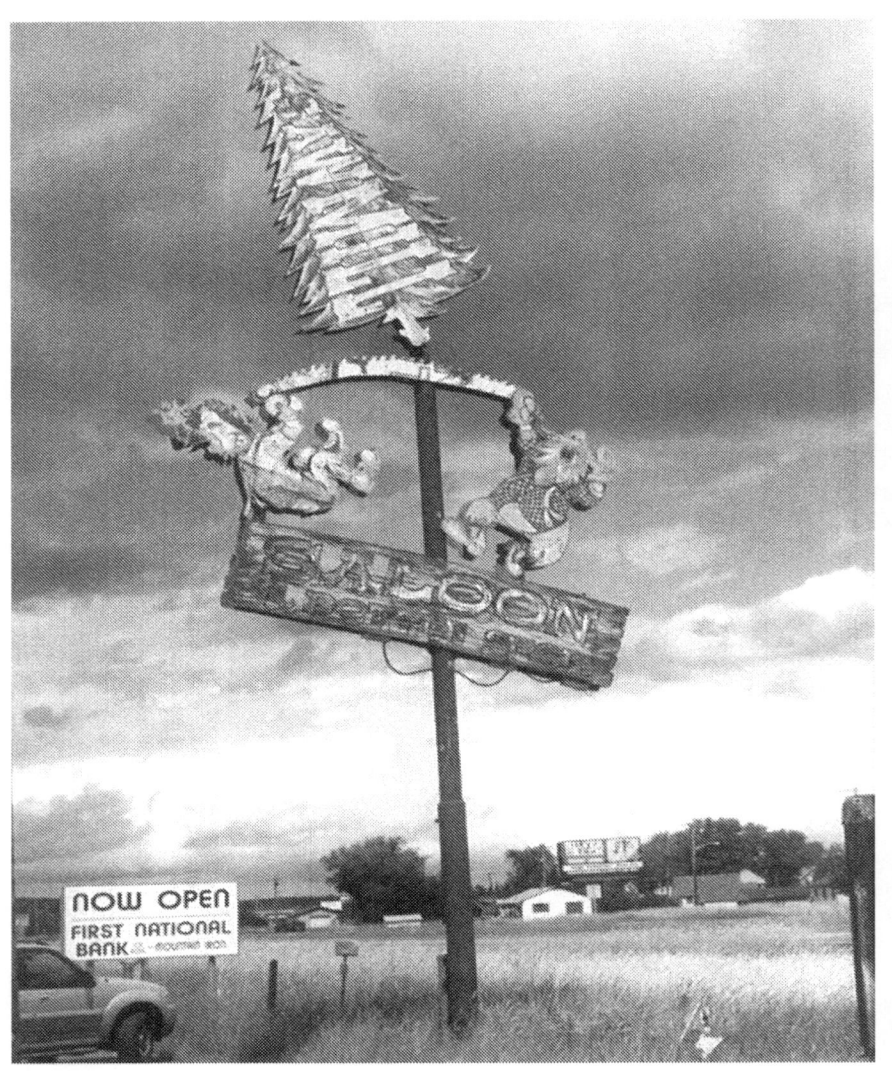

Old Sign; Virginia, Minnesota, 2006

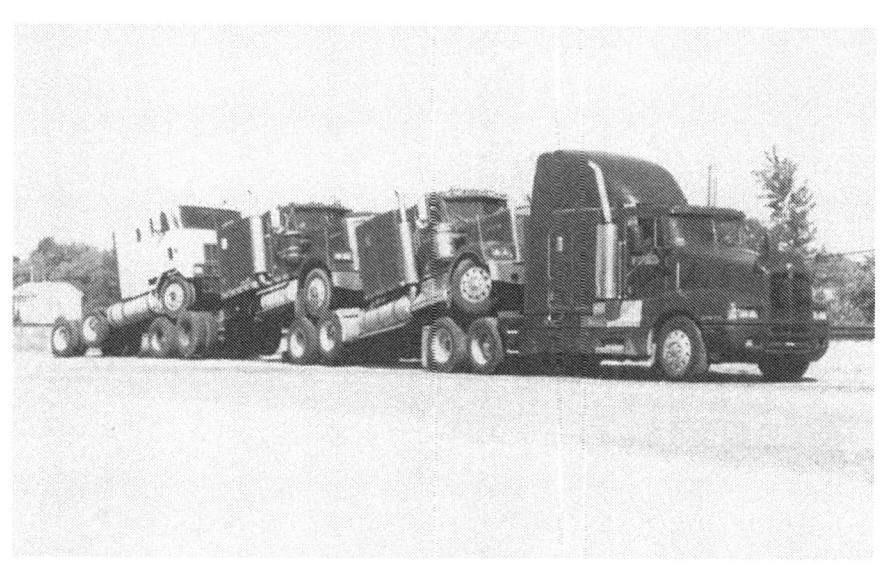

Piggy-Back Trucks; Marceline, Missouri, 1998

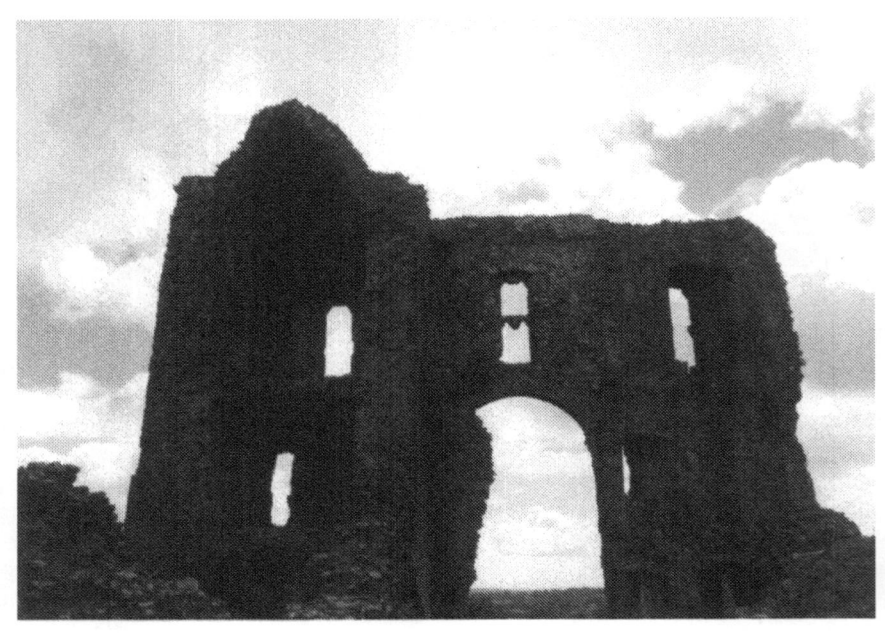

Welsh Castle Ruins, UK, 1988

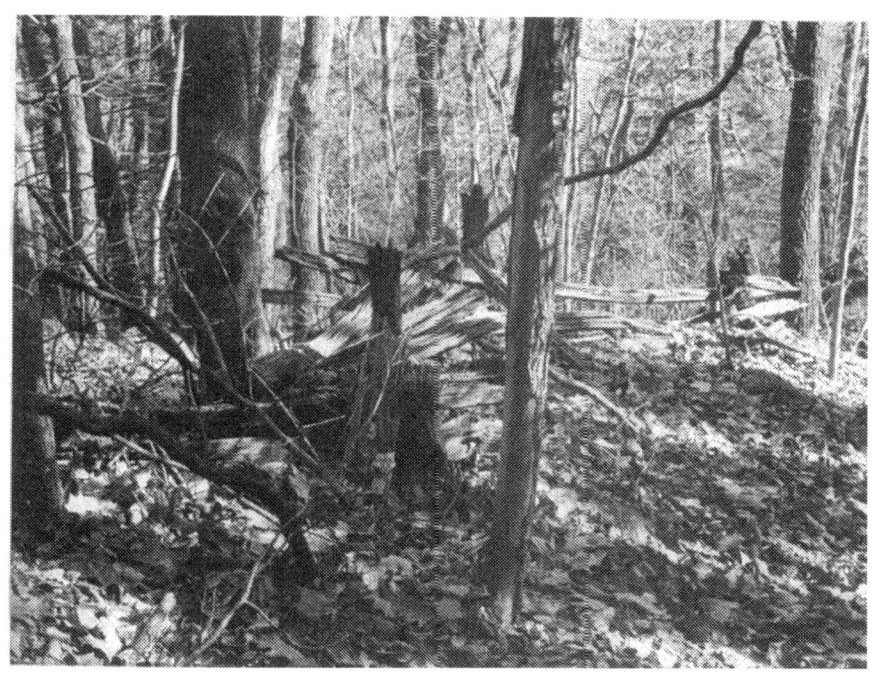

Rural Augusta County, Virginia, 1984

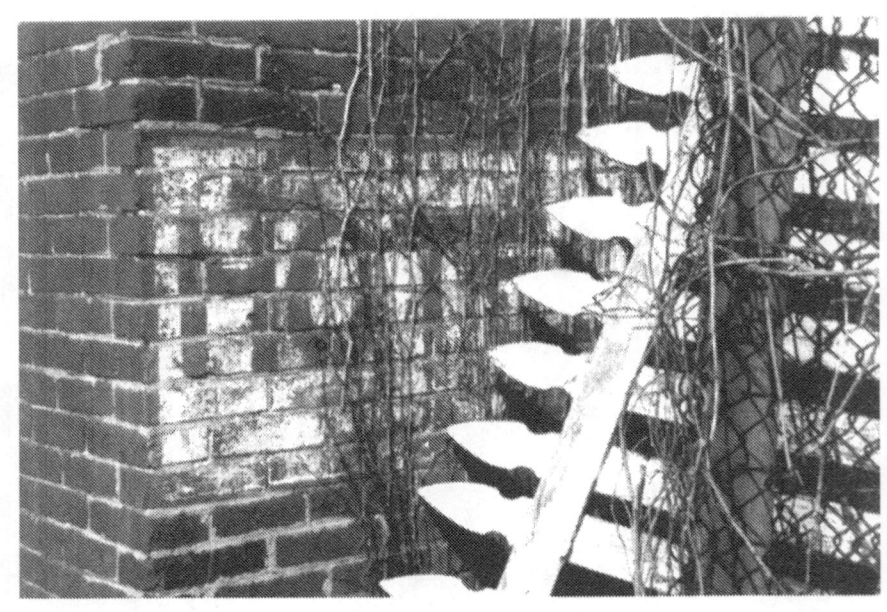

Abandoned Hotel, Boonville, Missouri, 2002

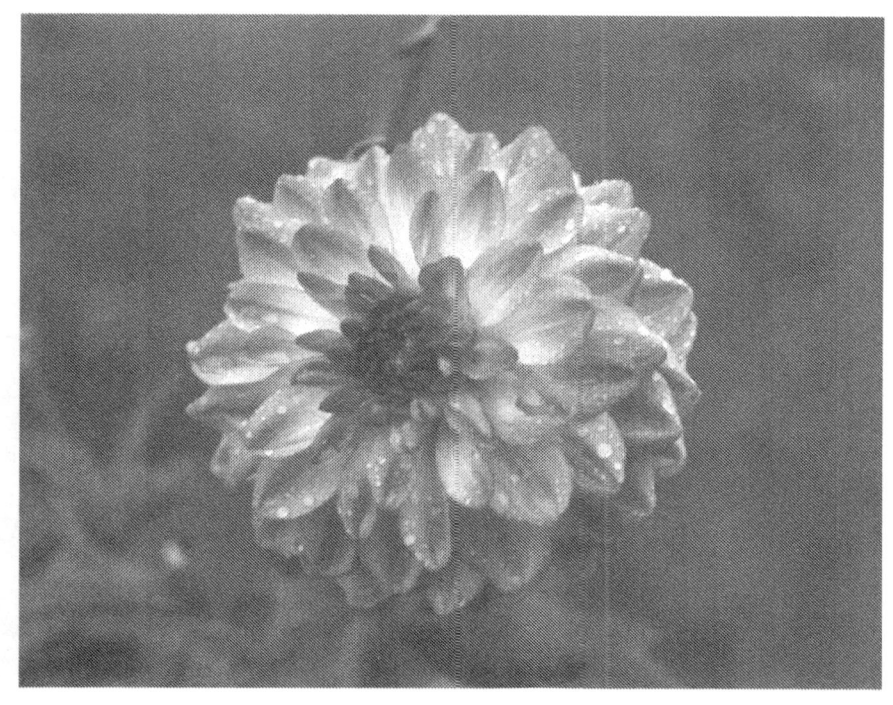

Flower After Rain; Moberly, Misscuri, 2005

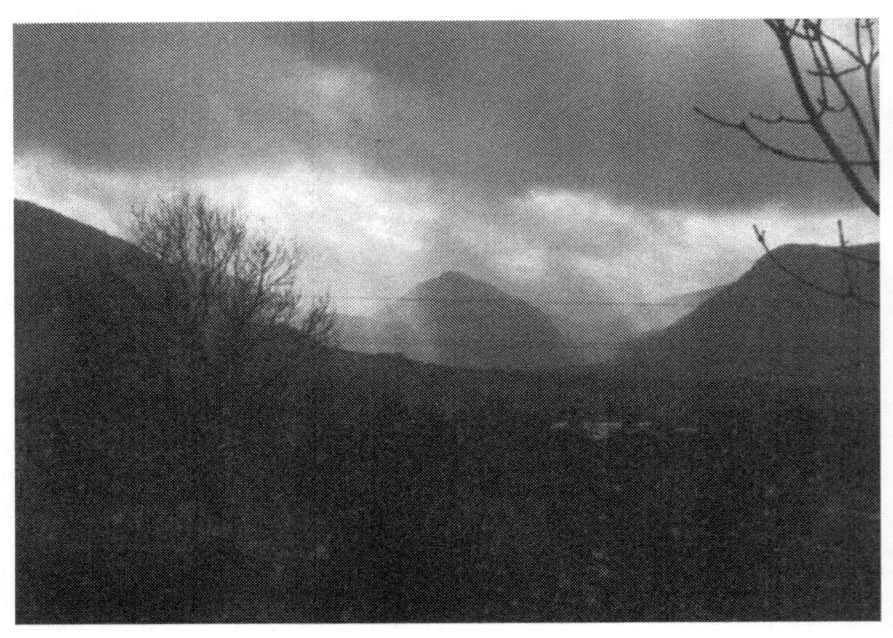

The Rain; Killarney, Ireland, 1989

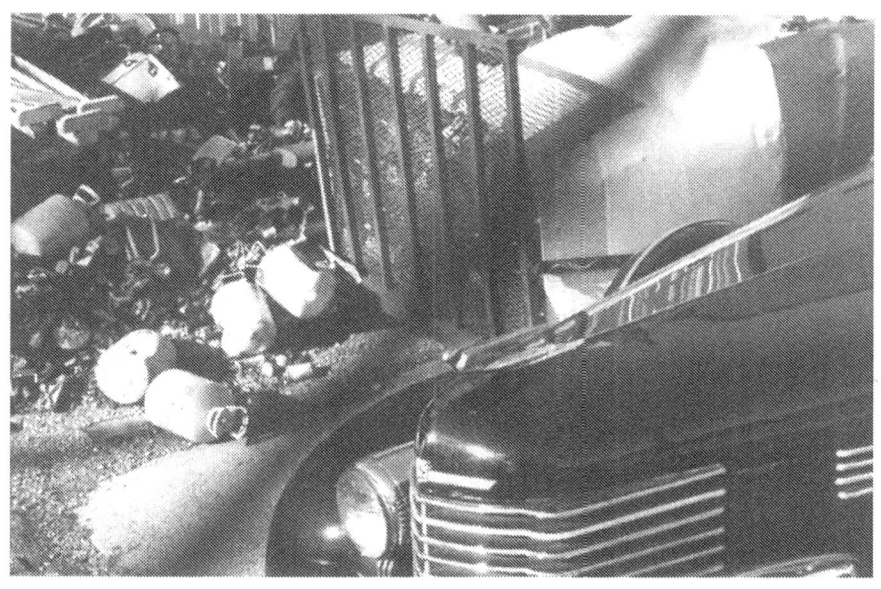

His Back Lot, Columbia, Missouri, 2006

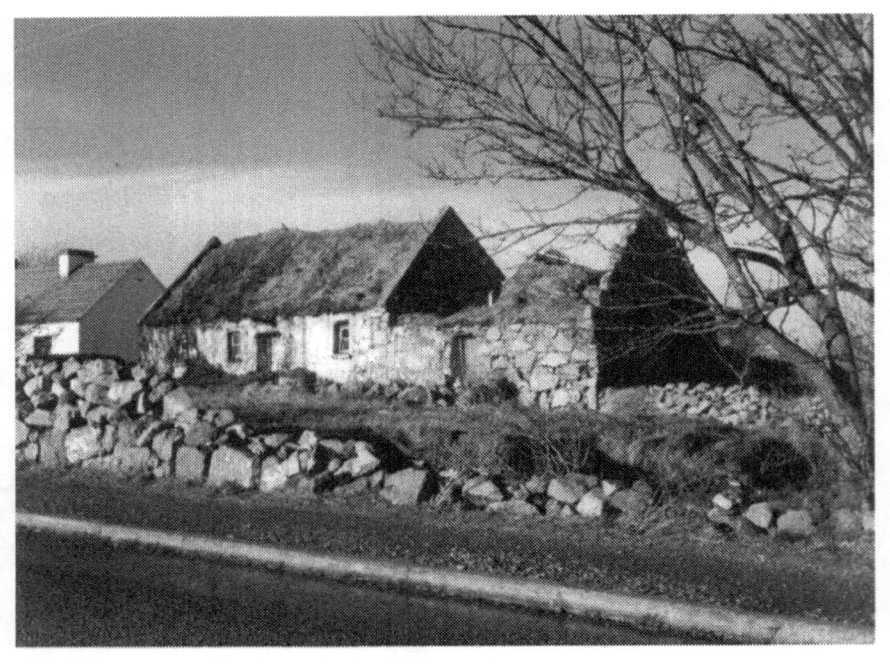

Cottages; Galway, Ireland, 1990

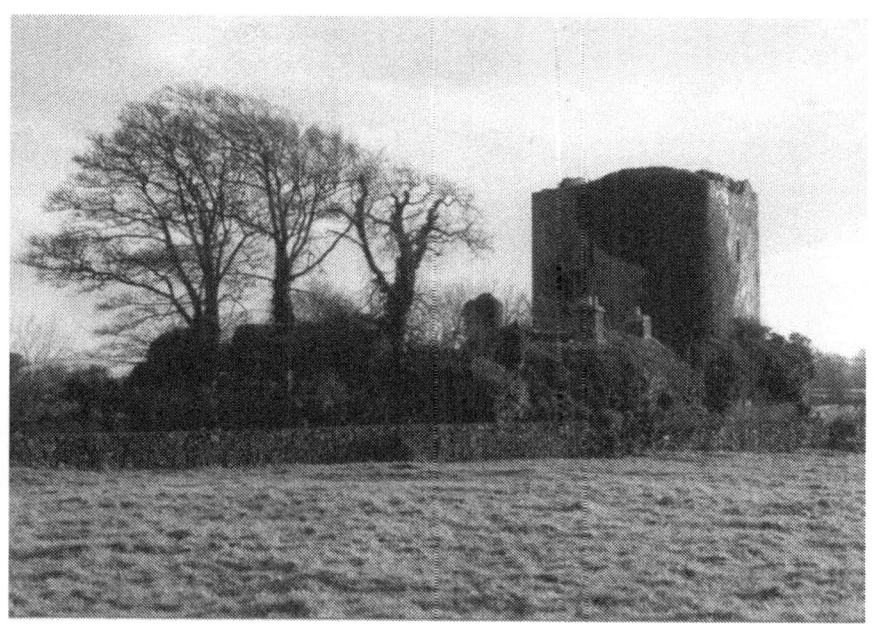

Village and Norman Keep, Ireland, 1990

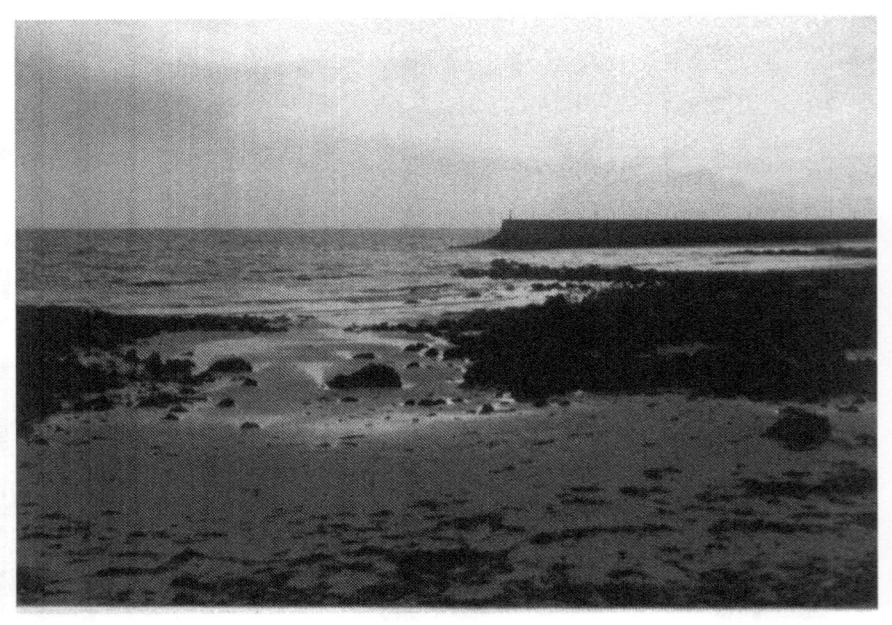

Galway Bay, Ireland; 1990
New York is just a few thousand miles over the horizon there...

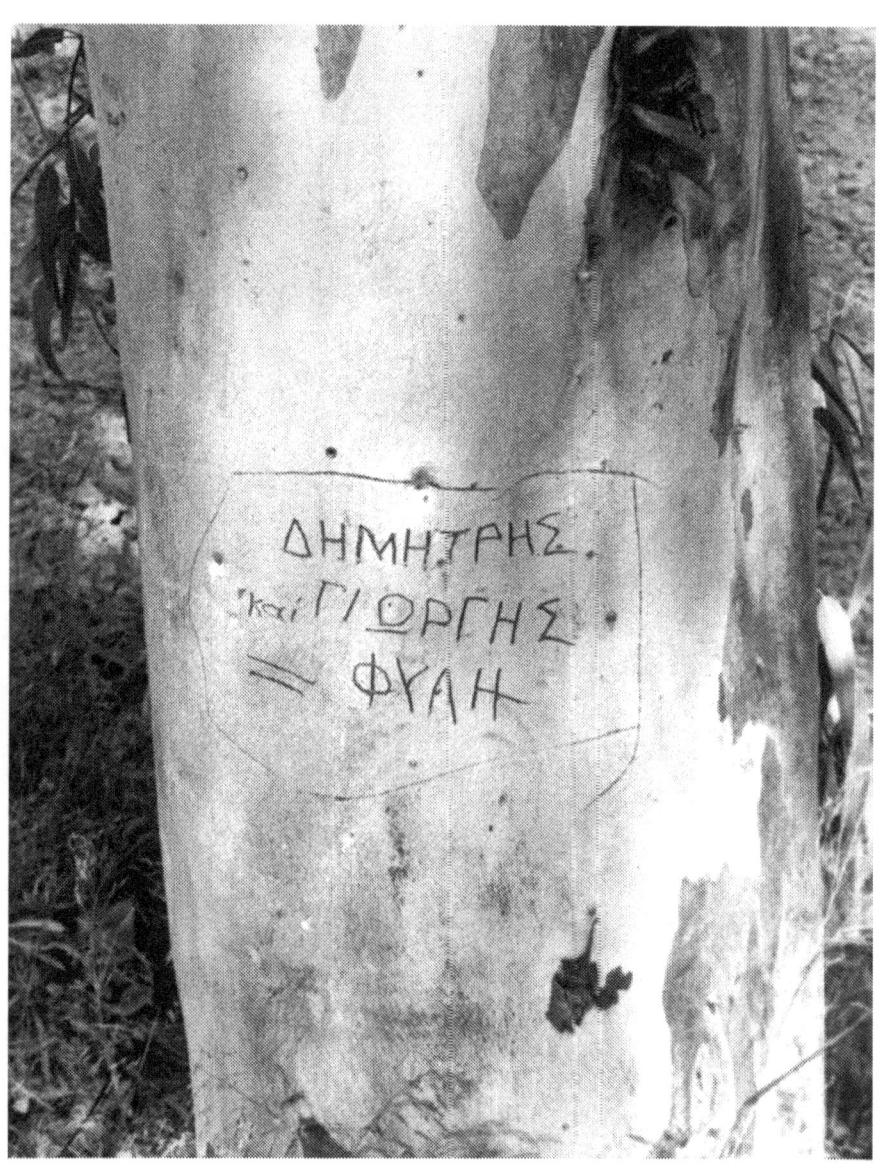

Graffiti in Greek; Rural South Crete, 1981

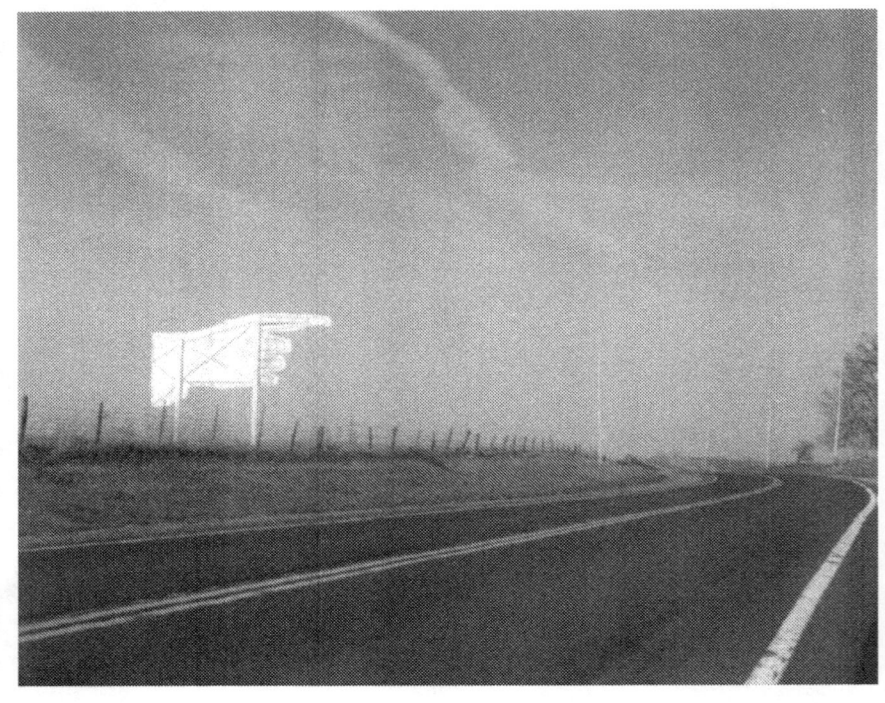

The Big Finger; Rural Missouri, 2006

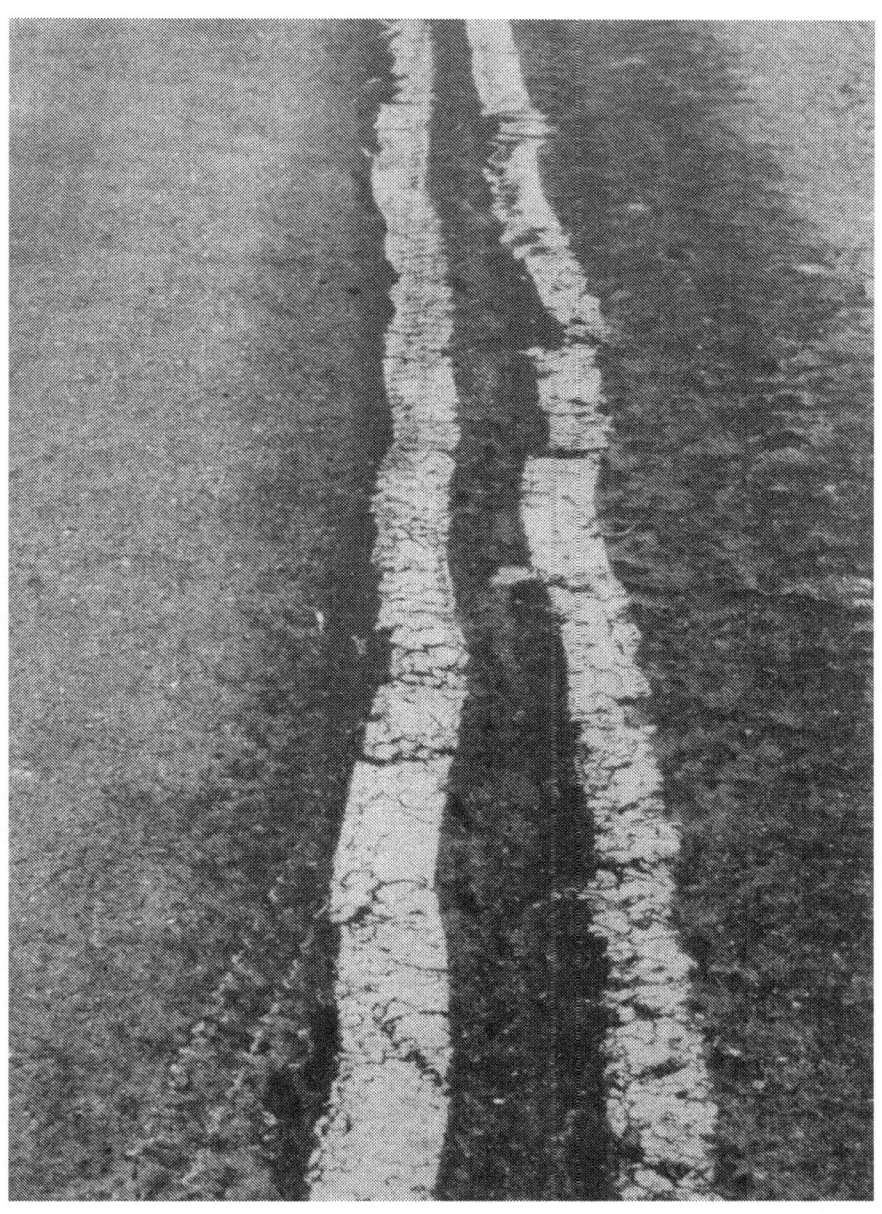

"What Have You Been Drinking?" Rural Missouri, 2006

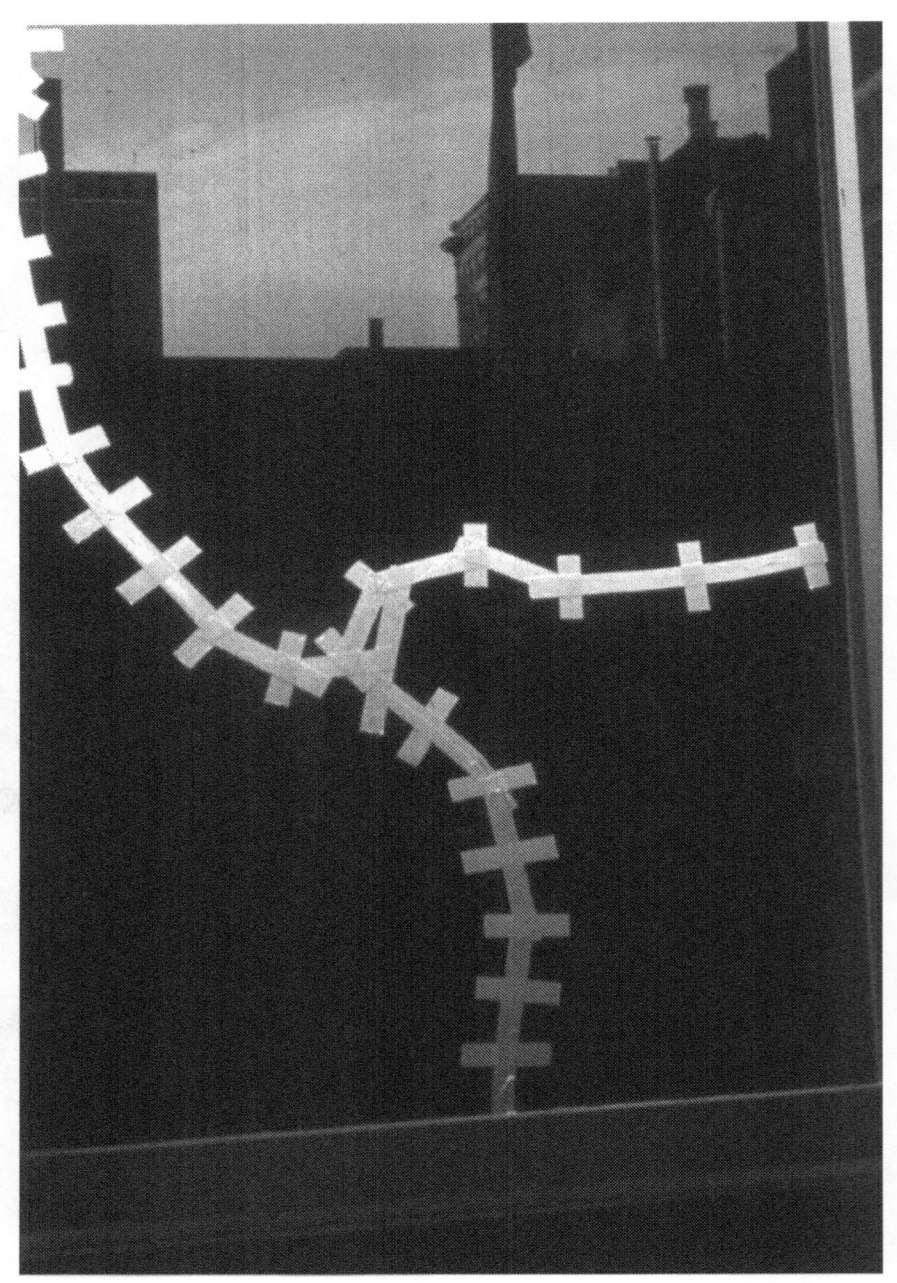

Duct Tape; Cincinnati, Ohio, 1969

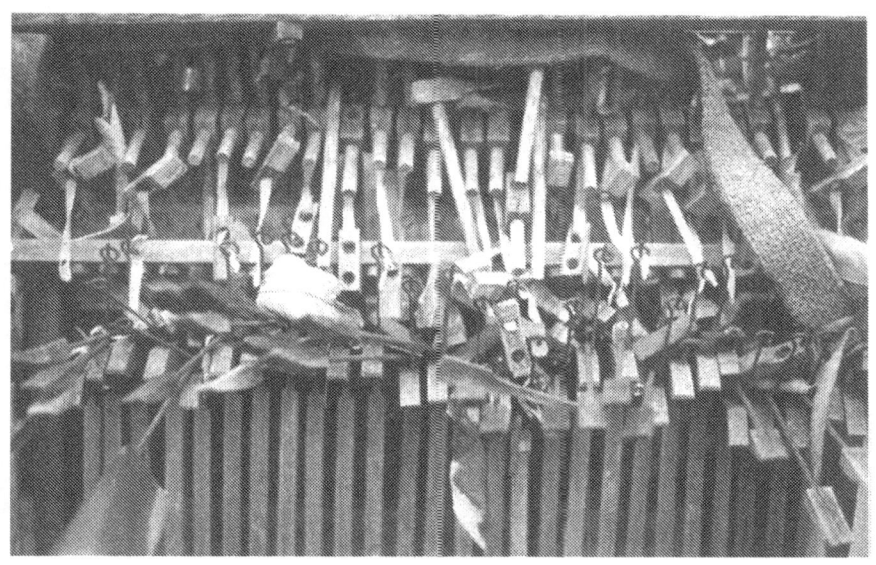

Piano Keys; Rural Missouri,2005

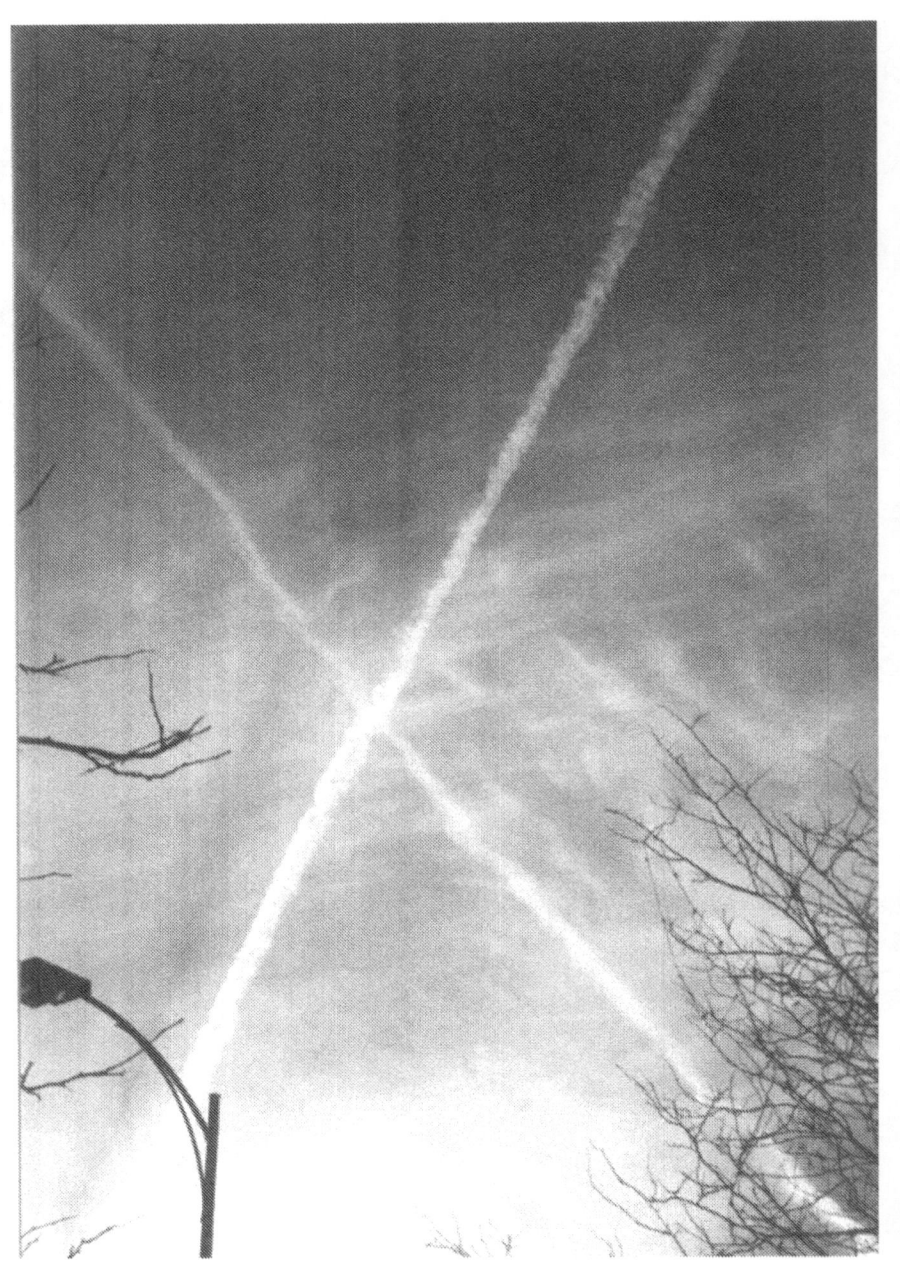

"X Marks The Spot," Columbia, Missouri, 1999

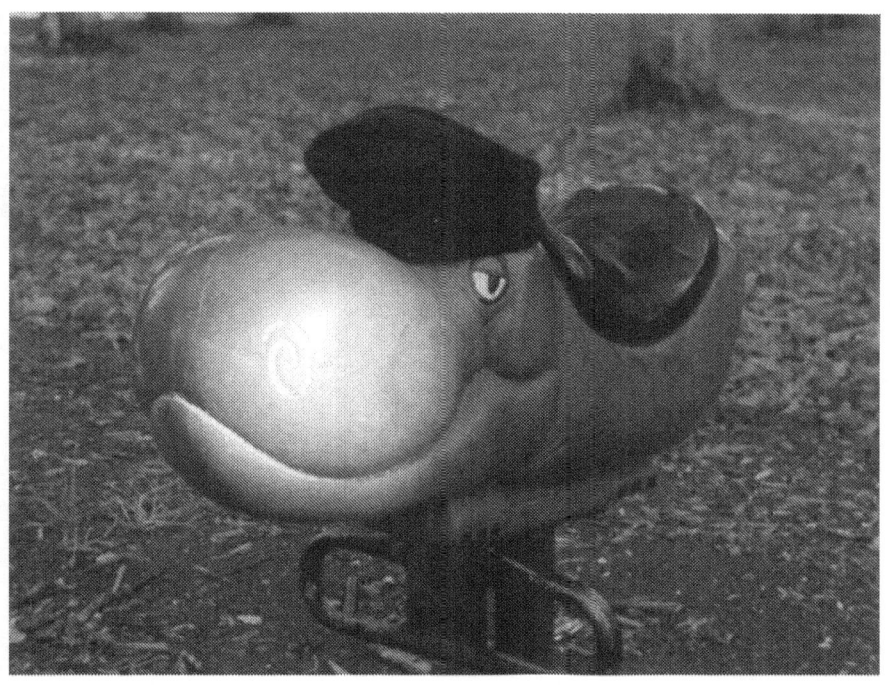

"That Satisfied Look," Moberly, Missouri, 2005

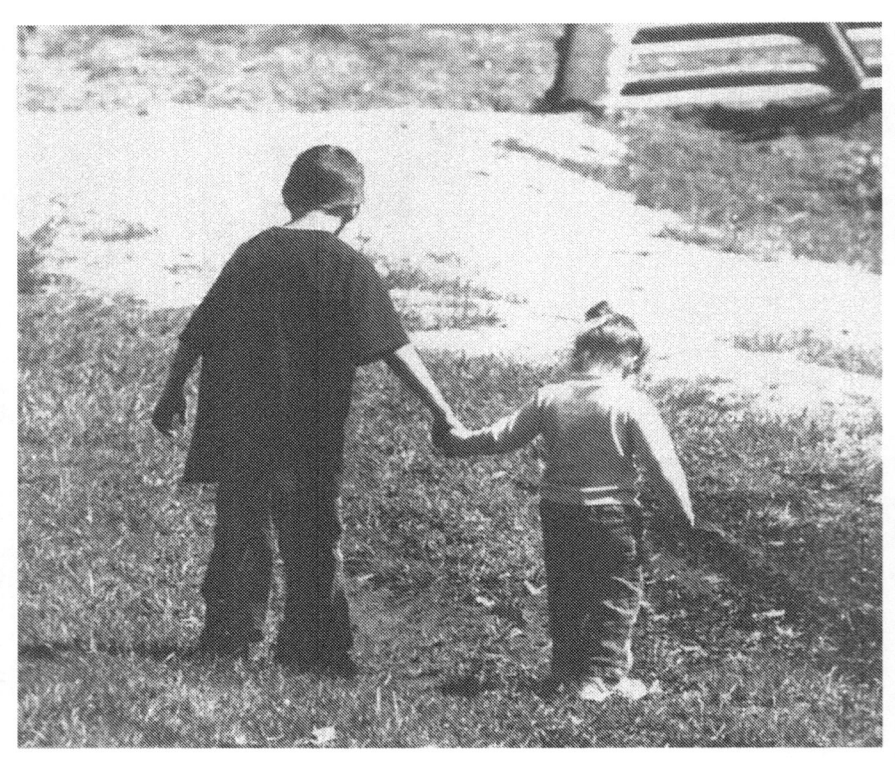

Untitled; Rural Missouri, 2005

Conclusion:

So what? Why THESE pictures? The world is full of dark, depressing images of dark, depressing things. Some will inevitably fall in front of your camera. Some photographers, good ones even, are sure that if they batter you with enough blood, enough sadness, enough death, you'll agree with them, and adopt their world view.

I don't agree. No, I think life is beautiful, and I love, most of all, the quest to catch artifacts of that beauty – so I can put them in front of you.

To an archaeologist (I am so trained), artifacts are the material remains, the "evidence," left by vanished cultures. Yes, people remember, people write, people tell stories of the past, but it is the material evidence that brings us closest to the truth.

"Carpe diem," said the Romans, "Seize the day." There is no better way to seize and hold a day, a time, a moment, than with a photograph.

So these are artifacts, material evidence of vanished moments. Are they art? I do not see myself as "manufacturer" of these images; I am a trapper, a hunter, a *papparazzo* of *bel canto* moments, of "lyrical documentary."

So, this collection? Welcome to my trophy room, my *apotheke.* These are my momentary artifacts.

Peter J. Nebergall manages the Columbia, MO-based freelance agency WORDS AND PICTURES. He has covered sports, fashion, archaeology, advertising, straight news, and war.

He has an extensive stock file; these images and others are for sale.
Contact: WORDS AND PICTURES
PO Box 754
Columbia, MO 65205
iusar4s@juno.com

STREET PHOTOG (2005) has more pictures, lessons learned, and the wisdom of Peter's teacher, Lester Wilson(an associate of Joe Rosenthal). It is available online, or from www.authorhouse.com

FACES OF PUNK (2003) is a full-color portfolio from Peter's research with Punkrockers and Gutter Punks. It is available from www.xlibris.com

HARD CORE: MARGINALIZED BY CHOICE (1997) was Peter's visual ethnography of Punkers. Published by Loompanics, it is out of print, but there should be a few copies left online. Try Amazon.

OUTERLOPER (2001) was a privately printed portfolio of B&W images and text. It is available from the author, at the above address.

Peter also has the novel THE COLOR OF HIS COAT, the short story collections SHEHARAZADE and LOST AND FOUND, and the textbooks VIOLENT SOCIETIES, GUERRILLA ANTHROPOLOGY, and FROM PICTOGRAPHIC TO COMPUGRAPHIC: WRITING FROM THE STONE AGE TO THE INFORMATION AGE, all at www.xlibris.com, and the story collection RAINDANCERS at www.authorhouse.com. Works ongoing include the story collections STORIES FROM THE REAL WORLD, THE THIRD BROTHER, and NUR SOLDATEN: STORIES FROM THE REICH.

----

www.ingramcontent.com/pod-product-compliance
Lightning Source LLC
Chambersburg PA
CBHW022005170526
45157CB00003B/1149